M000158483

TEACHING**THE**
CHRISTIAN**HOPE**

TEACHING**THE** CHRISTIAN**HOPE**

Unlocking Biblical Eschatology for the Expositor

DAVID**JACKMAN**

PROCLAMATION TRUST MEDIA

CHRISTIAN FOCUS

© Proclamation Trust Media 2004
ISBN 1-85792-518-1

Published in 2004
by
Christian Focus Publications
Geanies House, Fearn,
Ross-shire, IV20 1TW, Great Britain
with
Proclamation Trust Media,
Willcox House, 140-148 Borough High Street,
London, SE1 1LB, Great Britain.
www.proctrust.org.uk

www.christianfocus.com

Series Editor : William J U Philip

Cover design by Alister MacInnes

Printed and bound in Denmark by Nørhaven Paperback

All rights reserved. No part of this publication may be reproduced, stored in a retrieval system, or transmitted, in any form, by any means, electronic, mechanical, photocopying, recording or otherwise without the prior permission of the publisher or a license permitting restricted copying. In the U.K. such licenses are issued by the Copyright Licensing Agency, 90 Tottenham Court Road, London W1P 9HE

Contents

Preface
Introducing the 'Teaching' Series

Christian teachers and preachers constantly need encouragement
to keep on with the task of declaring God's truth to the church
and to the world, 'in season and out of season', whether people
will receive it, or not. It is a demanding responsibility to teach
the truth, the whole truth and nothing but the truth in a culture
which has ceased to believe in truth's very existence. But we also
need encouragement to do the job better; to keep on improving
our human talents and abilities, to develop new lines of thinking
about the relevant application of God's unchanging Word to
our contemporary context. Above all, we need to grow in our
faithfulness to what God has said and in our dependence on the
Holy Spirit to use the Word of God, to do the work of God,
through us.

That is the purpose behind the *Teaching* series from
Proclamation Trust Media. To date we have published *Teaching
Matthew* and *Teaching John*, which have drawn encouraging
responses, and so we are developing the series by focusing not
just on biblical books, but also on the challenge of preaching
the great doctrines of the faith. *Teaching the Christian Hope* is
therefore offered in order to encourage lively Bible teaching about

eschatology, the future hope that lies at the heart of the whole message of the gospel.

The hallmark of the series is that each book aims not merely to teach the readers the truth of God from Scripture, but also to offer real help towards them teaching this truth to others, through opening the Bible themselves. Though principally aimed at preachers who are preparing expository sermons, our hope is that Bible teachers in a variety of settings will gain practical help from the approach. To this end, each chapter is clearly divided into 'teachable' sections, with headings and sub-headings arranged suggestively for main teaching points or whole expositions. We trust that this will whet the appetite for further reflection and study, while at the same time helping crystallize thinking towards preparation of the sermon or Bible talk. Our goal is to stimulate a fresh excitement and desire among many for *Teaching the Christian Hope*.

William J U Philip
Series Editor

Introduction

Expository preaching and teaching must always be text-controlled, in that its *raison d'être* is to seek to understand the living and enduring Word of God, as written. Classically, this has rightly centred on systematic consecutive exposition of books, or parts of books, setting the material in its own context, within the book and thus within the Bible, as a whole. But how is doctrine to be taught? For the classic Bible expositor the answer has been (again rightly, I think) as and when it appears in the text. However, the challenge is then to prevent the constituent ingredients of a particular doctrine from overwhelming the text under consideration, rather than illuminating it. The net result can be an approach to exposition which takes only a sentence or verse in order to unpack its main doctrinal content, and proceeds to examine a particular ingredient of systematic theology rather than teach the contextualized content and purpose of this unique passage. What passes for expository preaching can then turn into lectures in systematic theology, which while truthful and no doubt edifying in their way, are nevertheless hard to digest, often mainly cerebral in content and can ultimately develop a culture of knowledge rather than understanding and obedience, in those who hear.

How then *is* doctrine to be taught? For there is no doubt that it needs to be, as well as learned and applied. One answer might be the thematic sermon, though even here I would want to encourage the use of a key passage, to function as a home-base, to ground the talk in exposition, and from which excursions to a few other parallel passages could profitably be made. The danger with this sort of approach is that it might degenerate into a concordance sermon, where a trail of verses is followed, as our fingers do the walking through the 'yellow pages' of Scripture. The more verses, the less penetrating comment is likely, and so the hearer finds it increasingly difficult to assimilate the avalanche of information, assess its significance or even begin to consider its application. This is a very difficult type of teaching to do well, in terms of its positive impact on the hearers' lives, although it is probably one of the easiest to prepare, in terms of gathering the material.

So, in this book, I have tried to identify six major themes connected with the Christian hope, in order to think about how to teach biblical eschatology. In each chapter I will suggest one or two major passages which could provide the foundational expository ingredient of the sermon. I will also suggest some of the key issues that need to be covered in dealing with the theme, to avoid either confusion or the failure to connect with the questions, uncertainties and doubts many believers experience in dealing with these areas. The perspective will always be firstly on motivating the teacher first, and then the hearers, rightly to handle and understand what Scripture clearly does say, and then to emphasise the immense benefit and strengthening to daily faith which a proper grasp of the certainties of our hope can bring every believer.

This is a book for Bible teachers, about dealing with what are often regarded as difficult and controversial areas of Scripture and therefore have tended to be avoided or ignored. It is not a comprehensive survey of all the issues bound up in the study of biblical eschatology, nor does it seek to answer the many tantalising questions the subject matter raises for our curiosity. Many scholars, far more able and erudite than I, have produced excellent work on the subject, to which the reader will be referred from time to time. This is a practical book, to stimulate Bible teachers to *want* to teach the Christian hope, and to give a few preliminary suggestions and ideas about how we might go about it. As such, I hope that it may prove helpful not only to pulpit preachers, but also to Bible-study group leaders, youth workers and even Sunday-school teachers, for teaching about eschatology is certainly under-represented in many of our programmes, across the strata of contemporary evangelical church life. It is not intended to do the work for the teacher, but to come alongside to help, encourage, and perhaps outline some possibilities.

It has been my privilege to teach much of the material here at the Crieff Ministers' Conference in Scotland and at conferences held under the auspices of the Proclamation Trust. I am very grateful to my friend and colleague, Dr William Philip, for many helpful suggestions, and to Kate Bailey and Nancy Olsen, whose valiant efforts in deciphering my original manuscripts and facilitating its editing, combined with their consistent enthusiasm for the project, mean that it has at least seen the light of day! To these and all others who have commented and from whom I have learned so much, my grateful thanks. My prayer is that those who read will be enthused and helped to declare the great certainties of a future, in Christ, which is as bright as the promises of God, for no message is more urgently needed in our dark and dying world. 'May the God of hope fill you with all joy and peace as you trust in him, so that you may overflow with hope by the power of the Holy Spirit' (Rom. 15:13).

David Jackman
London, February 2004

1

Hope for a Hopeless World

The Way In

One of the Bible teacher's main responsibilities is to relate the unchanging truth of Scripture to the life-situation of the hearers, which will inevitably vary, from time to time and place to place. This is not to say that the talk is simply to cater to the felt needs, or immediate demands, of those who listen. The Bible itself is totally realistic about this. 'For the time will come when men will not put up with sound doctrine. Instead, to suit their own desires, they will gather around them a great number of teachers to say what their itching ears want to hear. They will turn their ears away from the truth and turn aside to myths' (2 Tim 4:3-4). Such a time has undoubtedly come! The wise Christian leader is responsible for feeding God's people on the nourishment of the Bible, and there must be no trendy new diets allowed to substitute for that good food. But when there is weakness or sickness in the physical body, the appetite is often impaired, and it can require both dietary skill and attractive presentation of appropriate ingredients to coax the patient back to health. The pastor-teacher needs parallel wisdom and skill in dealing with the multitude of ailments which are suffered in the spiritual realm, so that God's truth can be assimilated and its nourishment digested.

The presenting symptoms in many congregations and individual Christians today are those of spiritual lethargy and depression. Catastrophic numerical decline, not only in nominal church attendance, but also in the number of active believers at work for Christ in our culture, have produced a long-term erosion of confidence, which can easily move into disillusionment and even despair. Many congregations are holding together only by virtue of a small committed core, whose average age increases, as their overall numbers decline. Sadly, the only remedy propounded seems so often to work the committed crew into the ground, loading more and more responsibilities upon them, not least the increasing financial demands of ministry provision, until the camel's back is inevitably broken. It is disturbing increasingly to come across committed older Christians, who having served faithfully for years have now decided that they have 'had enough', that it's time to have a rest, put up their feet and let somebody else do it all, irrespective of whether there is anybody to fill their shoes, or not. They have not been nurtured and cared for. Often they have not been considered, or valued. They have been running just above 'empty' on the spiritual fuel tank, perhaps for years, and the strain has been so great, combined with so little in the way of returns, that they have effectively decided that church involvement is something they can do without. This is a tragic waste of middle-aged potential through burn-out, every bit as desperate as the teens and twenties wastage through drop-out.

At root, the problem is a lack of hope. No amount of cajoling, beating-up support, or, alternatively, entertainment and indulging personal whims and fancies will get anywhere near dealing with the underlying malaise. It goes much deeper. For many Christians and their churches the unthinkable has happened, the bottom has fallen out of their boat. The gods of our culture seem to be in imperious command. You cannot be a Christian living in the real world, at the beginning of the third millennium, at least in the west, without asking what the church has to offer our society, before beginning even to consider how it might be done.

The answer, of course, is hope. But if so many Christians feel their situation is literally hope-less, in terms of the credibility of the historic, biblical faith in the modern world, not just at the intellectual level, but at the daily level of personal experience, nothing will change. The erosion may accelerate into disintegration, since although Christ is committed to building his church and no hostile powers can resist or overcome him (Matt 16:18), there is no guarantee in Scripture of that promise applying to any particular geographical location or period of history. Should it not be a priority, then, to put the uniqueness of our sure and certain hope in Christ back at the top of our teaching agenda?

Facing the challenge

Whenever we discover that a particular aspect of God's full-orbed revelation has been neglected or forgotten in our own lives, or within the wider context of our churches, it is often because its credibility is being particularly denied or dismissed by the 'spirit of the age', in the unbelieving world around us. Marxist sociological analysis of religion has penetrated deeply into our culture with its emphasis on belief as subjugation, formalised faith communities as a means of control and power over people, and its ridicule of heaven as 'pie in the sky when you die', truly 'the opiate of the masses'. Only, the masses have other opiates today, and certainly in the developed world, any emphasis on heaven rings hollow, because, as the song tells us, 'heaven is a place on earth'. The good life continues apace and for most of us our standard of living is higher than even our parents might ever have anticipated.

In spite of the vagaries of the markets, our overall wealth seems to be increasing. Technology continues to move forward at supersonic speed, offering possibilities beyond the wildest imagination of previous generations. There are massive events on a global scale, such as the 2004 Olympic Games in Athens, carried instantly across the world, which seem to hold out the prospect of a new age of unity, founded on the development of respect, tolerance and pride in human achievement. The war on terrorism continues, of course, but much of the world is hugely optimistic about the future. The commercial interests behind the ever-expanding mass media will ensure that the assessments we are constantly offered are as up-beat as possible.

We may not sing, as Swinburne did towards the end of the nineteenth century, 'Glory to man in the highest, for man is the master of things'. We may look back on the twentieth century and, seeing its horrors, realise the essentially flawed and fallen nature of the human race. But the up-and-coming generation does not generally think like that. They are not without hope, because they are being reared in a world where yesterday's unthinkable progress has become today's common reality. Everything is now possible. So we live and minister in a culture of impressive wealth and status, power and confidence. It is indeed a 'world without end', unless it is ended by our own mismanagement of the planet. Unless, as Christian communicators, we face these false confidences eye-to-eye, we shall always be speaking into a vacuum. From our culture's standpoint, the end of the church is a very likely probability, because it is so hopelessly out of date and irrelevant, but the end of the world is only the stuff of disaster movies and the wilder reaches of scientific speculation about collisions with asteroids.

And yet…! As I am writing this, through the post today, I have received some promotional literature with the following facts about the UK, published by the Samaritans. 'More people are on antidepressants than voted for Pop Idol.' 'Five million working days are lost due to stress, depression and anxiety in the UK and the Republic of Ireland each year.' 'Nearly twice as many people die by suicide each year as die in road accidents.' The gap between the glitzy, media-manufactured fantasy worlds and the hard reality of daily life for millions does nothing but widen. It should come as no surprise if the smiling, optimistic public face of popular culture masks a deep-seated cynicism and despair, which is characterised at its most extreme by hopelessness. Possibly the familiar response to the greeting, 'How are you?' as 'Oh, not so bad' or 'Can't complain, I guess' is much nearer to the daily experience of more people than we care to believe. That may be why materialism continues to grip us, because it offers us our only hopes.

Hope is therefore a major and urgent need, both within the church and outside it, so that the Christian pastor/teacher who determines to teach this area of God's revelation is certain to connect with one of the deepest seams of personal need, in our culture and so in our congregations. For the church is always far more conditioned by the prevailing climate of the culture around us, than we usually want to admit (Rom. 12:2). One of the most important reasons for the regular exercise of a teaching ministry is so that we resist the pressure of the world to squeeze our thinking into its mould and realign our mind-set, attitudes and priorities according to God's revealed truth, instead. When the Bible is controlling our thoughts and assessments, we shall see many parallel elements of Old Testament Babylon in our contemporary culture – its arrogant confidence, its addiction to idolatry, its domination and exploitation of the weak (read Isaiah 46 and 47), but also its inevitable judgment and ruin. Or Psalm

73 will help us to look at the apparent temporal prosperity of God's enemies in the light of eternity and what the writer describes as their 'final destiny' (17).

> As a dream when one awakes, so when you arise, O Lord, you will despise them as fantasies . . . Those who are far from you will perish; you destroy all who are unfaithful to you. But as for me, it is good to be near God. I have made the Sovereign LORD my refuge; I will tell of all your deeds (Ps. 73: 20, 27 & 28).

The psalmist's perspective – looking at the end point while involved in the process – is what helps us to understand the world from God's point of view. Then we can make right judgments about the use of our time, resources and energy, and about the focus of our whole lives.

It is time for us to begin our exploration of the nature of Biblical hope, which will occupy the rest of this chapter, in three sections. First, we shall take the longest possible view into the future of God's eternal kingdom and look at the ultimate focus of our hope, using Ephesians 1 as our key passage. Then we shall look at the practical applications of this truth to our present experience, as we explore how the certainties of the 'not yet' should impact life in the here and now, and especially how hope is related to faith. The chapter ends with a brief excursion into Romans 8 to provide another Biblical key to the practical implications of living in Biblical hope.

1. THE ULTIMATE FOCUS OF CHRISTIAN HOPE

In Ephesians 1 we discover a biblical perspective which should control all our thinking about the future:

> And God made known to us the mystery of
> his will according to his good pleasure, which
> he purposed in Christ, to be put into effect
> when the times will have reached their
> fulfilment – to bring all things in heaven and
> on earth together under one head, even Christ
> (Eph. 1:9 & 10)

In other words, the previously hidden secret of God's inscrutable will has now been revealed. The whole subsequent history of the coming of the Lord Jesus and the progress of the gospel leads up to this great climax. This is the focus which is dominant all the way through human history and to which climax God is irresistibly working everything together – that everything in all creation will be brought in unity under one head, even Christ.

If we look back at the verses which immediately precede this, we can observe that the phrase 'in Christ' comes up again and again:

> Praise be to the God and Father of our Lord
> Jesus Christ, who has blessed us in the heavenly
> realms with every spiritual blessing *in Christ*. For
> he chose us *in him* . . . he predestined us to be
> adopted as his sons through Jesus Christ . . . *In
> him* we have redemption through his blood
> (Eph. 1: 3-5, 7).

Paul is saying that the Christ through whom God chose and predestined us to be adopted as his children, the Christ in whom we have redemption and the forgiveness of sins – who is defined by his work on the cross and by his glorious resurrection – that Christ is the ultimate purpose and focus of God's plan for the whole universe.

The uniting of everything in heaven and on earth will therefore be in and through this Christ, the Christ of our redemption. He is the one in whom God chooses to sum up the entire cosmos. He is the one who restores harmony to the created order. But he is not just the instrument or the agent of that restoration; he is the focus, the centre point of it all. Everything points to, and actually comes to, its fulfilment in Christ. So all the alienated elements of the fractured universe are being brought together under one head, even Christ.

The cosmic battle

In these verses, the apostle Paul speaks about God bringing 'all things in heaven and on earth' under the headship of Christ. That means the totality. He divides the whole of creation into the 'heavenlies' and the 'earthlies'. While there is no absolute polarity between the spiritual and the physical in the New Testament, it is convenient for us to think in terms of living our life in the earthly sphere, but as citizens of the heavenly kingdom.

Over both these areas and therefore over the whole of human existence, created beings have resisted and rebelled against God's sovereign rule. In Ephesians 6:12 we read that our struggle is not against flesh and blood but against the rulers, authorities, the powers of this dark world, against the spiritual forces of evil in the 'heavenly realms'. This phrase cannot simply be equated with heaven, where Christ is, because there can be no spiritual forces of evil there. Rather, we should understand the whole realm of spiritual energies where the devil and his demons are constantly at work against the will of God and the angel hosts of heaven who are loyal to him. Although Christ has already won the victory at the cross, nonetheless a battle continues in this world until Jesus returns. Paul talks about it in terms of the 'heavenly realms', but we experience it in our daily struggles as Christians on earth.

The importance of what he is saying, however, is that wherever there are hostile powers ranged against God, whether they are Satan and his hordes, or rebellious human beings under his influence, all of those powers will ultimately come under one head, even Christ. They will be forced to submit to Christ and his eternal rule, in the everlasting Kingdom of the heavens.

The restoration of all things

God's plan is for a glorious restoration, the appointed climax, the full measure of the times when everything is complete and the goal will be achieved. That will see Jesus ruling and reigning supreme over everything. That is the ultimate focus of history, but this great plan is already under way, already operative in the church, because of the death and resurrection of Christ:

> That power is like the working of his mighty strength, which he exerted in Christ when he raised him from the dead and seated him at his right hand in the heavenly realms, far above all rule and authority, power and dominion, and every title that can be given, not only in the present age but also in the one to come. And God placed all things under his feet and appointed him to be head over everything for the church, which is his body, the fullness of him who fills everything in every way (Eph. 1:19-23).

Paul's point is that this is already happening. The final summing up of the universe in Christ as God's final goal has not yet been realised, but already that mighty power is demonstrated in the resurrection of Jesus and in his ascension to the right hand of the Father where he rules in sovereign power.

Already it is seen in the fact that now he is the head of the church, his body, where he rules in grace, love and truth. Indeed, the argument of Ephesians 2:11-22 is that in the breaking down of the divisions between Jewish and Gentile believers in Christ, so that the united church is 'one new man', the world is being given a present demonstration and evidence of the nature of the ultimate climax of history.

This great climax of history is not something that is going to appear unheralded or unprecedented 'out of the blue'; it is the logical conclusion of everything that God is doing now. All that we see already of the signs of his sovereign rule will come to their fruition when Christ appears in power and glory, when the whole created order will find itself under one head, even Christ.

As we explore our teaching of this uniquely Christian hope, we must keep this biblical focus on the Lord Jesus. It is not the doctrine of the last things, so much as Jesus ruling as king forever, that is the subject. Christ is the key to eschatology – it is all about his sovereign rule, and eschatology is the key to understanding the ultimate purpose of the whole Bible. So, this forward-looking in faith to the future is a distinctively *Christian* position and it is what the Bible means by the word *hope*.

It follows therefore that to be without Christ in this world is to be literally hope-less both now and in the world to come. The Gentile world of the church to which Paul is writing in Ephesus, in Asia Minor, is a world which he describes in Chapter 2:12 as being 'without hope, because it is without God'. So, let us put these two ideas together. The Christian's great hope is that Jesus will be exalted above everything, that he will reign as King of Kings and Lord of Lords throughout the aeons of eternity. Everything will be under his feet. But if we do not have God in this world, we shall remain separate from Christ, and so we condemn ourselves to be without this hope.

2. THE PRESENT EXPERIENCE OF CHRISTIAN HOPE

The blessings of the gospel bring with them both a redemption and an elevation of our fundamental human instincts and desires. Becoming a Christian does not make one less of a human being, but much more in that one is now spiritually alive, where before there was deadness. Rather than cancelling out our individual desires, and putting us all through the same mincing machine, the gospel redeems and elevates our personal, human characteristics to shape each of us into a unique representation of the likeness of Christ. It redeems all that God has made us as unique individuals, and elevates each of us to be able to reflect individually the Lord Jesus, whom we love and serve.

Hope is one of those human characteristics which God has built into us. So it is no surprise to recognise that hope rings bells with us at very deep levels of our being. It is observable in every human society that we are creatures of possibility, of hope. We do not appear in the world as finished articles, we influence our futures, we take responsible decisions, and much of our human life revolves around potentially realisable hopes. There is nothing wrong in that, although we have to recognise that sometimes those hopes are utopian in the extreme and sometimes they are just dream factories. Our problem is that we can become cynical about hope because our hopes in this world have so often been disappointed. Human hope, in this world, always has an element of uncertainty. But hope is the essence of humanity and the gospel is not against that, rather the gospel fulfils it. In teaching these realities it is always helpful to use everyday illustrations which people can easily identify with. So let me suggest one which may be useful in stressing the difference between true Christian hope and the down-valuing of the Word in everyday speech. Let's imagine that I am going to conduct a wedding service next Saturday. I turn up for the rehearsal on Friday night and after taking everyone through their paces, I say to the bridegroom, 'Well, I hope the sun shines tomorrow.' Now that is an expression of a pious wish that something nice might happen, but on the basis of the usual English summer, the likelihood may be 50-50 or worse. That is the way we tend to use the word *hope* today: it would be nice but it is unlikely.

However, supposing I then turn to the bride and say, 'And by the way I hope he turns up tomorrow', pointing to the bridegroom, she may well reply 'I certainly hope he does', by which she does not mean, 'Well, it would be nice but it's pretty uncertain'. She means that on the basis of all she knows up to this point, she is confident about what she does not yet know and what has not yet happened. That is Christian hope. It is not the 'wouldn't it be nice, but it probably won't' kind of hope. It is on the basis of what God has already accomplished and revealed that I am confident about what I do not yet have. That is our present experience.

A hope that is certain

It would be helpful to enable our hearers to think about how this hope works in our lives. It is the corollary of believing that there is a living God who has made the world and who is always active in that world – God who is sovereign, who is working out his best purposes, which are good, gracious and loving for his people—and that our future is certain. When we read Paul's words to the Ephesian Christians, 'Remember that you were separate from Christ, without hope and without God in the world', we see the connection. If you are in this world without the knowledge of that God, you have no hope, because ultimately God will bring you to his judgment throne and that will be a hopeless situation. A world without God is a world without purpose and a world without meaning.

However, when we become Christians we realise that the world has a future guaranteed by the sovereign God who made and sustains it. He is going to do something with it, and it is a future which is more certain, even though it is at present unseen, than any of the things we see around us. It will never prove to be a disappointment, because it is assured by the promise and character of this faithful, unchanging God. That is why the Bible is full of hope.

The New Testament demonstrates the realisation of the hope of the Old Testament. In the Old Testament, the sons of Abraham awaited the fulfilment of the covenant promise that God would be their God and they would be his people, and that they would be a great and blessed nation in the land he would give them. Eventually, having been brought out of Egypt through the Exodus, they were brought into the land of promise under Joshua's leadership. There, they hoped that they might be prosperous and grow, and under the kingship of David and Solomon it seemed that it might be happening. But following the division of the kingdom and because of Israel's persistent unfaithfulness to God, he condemned them to be taken into exile. Yet, their hope in God's promises remained, that one day the Messiah would come and that God would break in and initiate his new kingdom. It was all about hope in a faithful God, which is why the New Testament inheritors of those promises to Abraham continue to wait in hope. We are expecting the return of our king, looking forward to the new heaven and the new earth in which righteousness dwells.

The ingredients of hope

We are now in a position to summarise the three main constituents of our distinctive Biblical hope.

1. Expectation about the future

God has drawn back the curtain and shown us, at least in a measure, what he is going to do. We are expectant about it. It is exciting, and it motivates us. This forward focus is summed up in 2 Cor. 1:20, 'no matter how many promises God has made, they are 'Yes' in Christ'. This is the developmental line of biblical theology and salvation history throughout the Scriptures from Genesis to Revelation. So much has been fulfilled already in Christ and the gospel, as God's kingdom has already broken into our world, and yet so much still awaits fulfilment. That is why we can define ourselves as people who belong to the future. It is that forward impetus which becomes central to the apostolic preaching of the gospel in the Acts, with its emphasis on the resurrection, because the resurrection of Jesus is *the* great sign of the hope that will be ours when we are raised to life with him.

2. Trust in God's promise

Because we trust his person, we know that he is faithful, that he has forgiven us, that his fellowship with us is real, that he answers our prayers and that he changes our lives. Faith opens the door to the personal, experiential reality of all these blessings of the gospel in the 'here and now'. Those who know that God is to be trusted, who put their hope in him, therefore gain new strength: 'they who wait for the Lord shall renew their strength' (Is. 40:31). They put on new suits of clothes, which are characterised by their hope in every situation of life in this world, knowing that,

> 'God …acts on behalf of those who wait for him' (Is. 64:4).

3. Patient waiting

This is the present experience of our hope, though it is not the sort of waiting we face in a rail delay, where we sit in the waiting room for hours but do not know whether the train is coming or not. This is a waiting experience of frustration, caused by uncertainty. Rather, it is the waiting which our children experience as December 24th approaches, when under the Christmas tree there may be that present which looks as though it could be the right shape! This patient (and sometimes impatient!) waiting is based on the expectation and trust mentioned above. It is not so much a time concept as an attitude of confidence about the future, 'I know it is going to happen'.

Yet, although we are expectant and confident about the future, we should not be surprised to find that the world around us finds all this really difficult to accept. Again, the point can be helpfully made by use of an illustration. The evangelist David Watson used to tell the story of a Christian man whose wife had died. A few weeks later he met, in the street, a friend who had not heard this news. In the course of their conversation the friend, who was not a Christian, asked, 'And how's your wife?' 'Oh,' said the Christian, 'she's in heaven'. The friend was shocked and embarrassed. 'Oh,' said the friend, 'I am sorry'. Then, thinking that wasn't the right thing to say, had a second stab at it and said, 'Oh, I am glad'. But realising that wasn't quite appropriate either, his third and final attempt was, 'Oh, I am surprised!'

That is how the world has to deal with our hope. It has no categories to make sense of it, because Jesus is unique. But, for those of us who do know Christ, eternal life is the heart of our hope, and the resurrection of Jesus is its proof. Effectively, the New Testament keeps on reminding us, 'Your Saviour has risen from the dead, never to die again, and because you are in Christ, that gives you a destiny. You are united to him by faith, and so you are part of the destiny of redeemed humanity, which is full of hope.'

Hope derived from faith

Unfortunately, I have not been able to trace the origin of this quotation, but someone has said, 'Hope is listening to the music of the future, and faith is dancing to that music in the present'. I think that is terrific. Obviously, hope and faith are very closely related. Indeed, at times they seem almost interchangeable. But what is their relationship to one another and how does this symbiosis actually work, in practice?

In his *Institutes of the Christian Religion* John Calvin has this wonderful paragraph about faith and hope:

> In the one word hope is nothing more than the expectation of those things which faith previously believes to have been truly promised by God. Thus, faith believes that God is true, hope expects that in due season he will manifest his truth. Faith believes that he is our father, hope expects that he will always act the part of a father towards us. Faith believes that eternal life is given to us, hope expects that it will one day be revealed. Faith is the foundation on which hope rests, hope nourishes and sustains faith. (*Inst. III* c.2)

Faith cannot continue to exist without hope, and hope cannot exist without faith in God's promises and in the faithful God who will fulfil them. Our present experience, then, is that our hope is derived from faith, and is worked out in love. That is why the great enduring trilogy of the New Testament consists of faith, hope, and love (1 Cor. 13:13).

Because we are creatures of the here and now, however, people generally do not want to live in faith and hope. We want it all now. We want to see it now. All around us we are told that 'Seeing is believing. Show me it and I'll believe it'. But the Bible says, 'believing is seeing'. If you believe you will see, but if you wait to see before you believe, you won't be believing. Faith and hope take the promising word of the faithful God and build on the certainty of that, even though much of it by definition is not yet ours.

Many of us, at one time or another, have probably been attracted by the idea that we might like to have everything now and not have to wait for the 'not yet'. When I was a young Christian, there was a lot of teaching around about how one might rise above temptation and live a perfectly godly life, free from sin. It was not called perfectionism, but that is what it really was, as though there was some life-changing experience you could have which would lift you out of the struggle of having to go on believing, and place you above all those problems in undisturbed peace and rest. There has always been teaching like that in the church. Spurgeon is reputed to have said that he had only once met a 'perfect' man and he was a perfect nuisance! It surfaces in our day in some aspects of the healing movement and in the prosperity gospel, which promises that if only your faith is strong enough and you believe hard enough you can be infinitely healthy, wealthy and wise in this world.

But such beliefs destroy hope. I think it is fascinating that Paul says in 1 Cor. 15:19, 'If in this life only we have hoped in Christ, we are of all men most to be pitied.' That's true, isn't it? If this is the best it gets, aren't we to be pitied? There has got to be more than this as the fruit of the great redemptive work of Christ on the cross. So we must not fall for the false teaching that says, 'You can pull all of the "not yet" into the now if only you have enough faith.' Our personal experience now is enjoying all the blessings God has given us through the gospel (revisit Ephesians 1), but also holding on in hope and faith knowing that the best is yet to be and that the 'not yet' is even more glorious than what we presently experience.

3. THE PRACTICAL IMPLICATIONS
OF CHRISTIAN HOPE

I want to end this chapter by looking at the practical implications of all this as they are highlighted in some of the verses of Romans 8.

> I consider that our present sufferings are not worth comparing with the glory that will be revealed in us. The creation waits in eager expectation for the sons of God to be revealed. For the creation was subjected to frustration, not by its own choice, but by the will of the one who subjected it, in hope that the creation itself will be liberated from its bondage to decay and brought into the glorious freedom of the children of God. We know that the whole creation has been groaning as in the pains of childbirth right up to the present time. Not only so, but we ourselves, who have the firstfruits of the Spirit, groan inwardly as we wait eagerly for our adoption as sons, the redemption of our bodies. For in this hope we were saved. But hope that is seen is no hope at all. Who hopes for what he already has? But if we hope for what we do not yet have, we wait for it patiently. In the same way, the Spirit helps us in our weakness. We do not know what we ought to pray for, but the Spirit himself intercedes for us with groans that words cannot express. And he who searches our hearts knows the mind of the Spirit, because the Spirit intercedes for the saints in accordance with God's will.

> And we know that in all things God works for
> the good of those who love him, who have
> been called according to his purpose. For those
> God foreknew he also predestined to be
> conformed to the likeness of his Son, that he
> might be the firstborn among many brothers.
> And those he predestined, he also called; those
> he called, he also justified; those he justified,
> he also glorified (Rom. 8:18-30).

This is the summary of what we have been looking at and the key to our 'forward movement'. Paul's point in verse 18 is that suffering is not abnormal, nor is it necessarily a direct satanic intervention. It is normal life in this world, 'our present sufferings' as he describes them. They are the legacy of Adam's sin, and we have added to that inheritance by our rebellion. The only place where it will not be like that is this glorious new creation of the 'not yet', the heavenly fulfilment.

Crying out for something better

The powerful work of the Holy Spirit within the believer is, as the preceding verses have said (15-17), that we are crying out to God, 'Abba', as our father, in the midst of all of this, because we know that we belong to him, and that we are members of a family which has its true fulfilment in a new creation context. So, Christians do not expect to be airlifted out of what the fallen creation is going through, but the Spirit helps us to understand what it all means. Our spiritual instinct is to cry out for something better. That is a right instinct. We are people of hope, people who look to the future.

As verse 18 says, there is a glory that will be revealed *in* us, not just *to* us. We are going to be part of that glory, transformed into the likeness of the Lord Jesus. It is only on the basis of the gospel that we share Paul's wonderful expectation, but that gospel relating to every believer, will produce in all of us that same experience of glory, of likeness to the Lord Jesus.

It is a great encouragement to know that when we groan, when we long for something better, feeling that even the best things in this world do not satisfy us, we are being biblical Christians. One nineteenth-century hymn puts it like this:-

> 'I thank thee too that all our joy is touched with pain,
> That shadows fall on brightest hours and thorns remain,
> So that earth's bliss may be our guide,
> And not our chain.'

One of the reasons why God lets us experience present suffering is so that we learn that we are citizens of another country. Then we come to realise that this fallen world, with all its inevitable suffering, is in fact a staging post on the way to glory.

The redemption of creation

The whole creation waits in eager expectation for the sons of God to be revealed (19). That stresses both our own impatience and the creation's impatience. It is as though the whole created order is longing for it to be put right. As verse 20 says, the creation was subjected to frustration, and indeed in Genesis 3:13, the very earth is cursed because of human sin. But this is not the end of the story for 'it is subjected to frustration in hope that the creation itself will be liberated from its bondage to decay' (20). Creation too will be brought into the same glorious freedom that Christ gives us, recreated as new heavens and a new earth in which righteousness dwells. This gives us great hope, because creation has a purpose in God's plans, right from Genesis 1, through history, and on to its redeemed form in the future. All that we were ordained to do in the world might have its frustrations now, but we can be joyful that our rule with Christ in the new creation will be fruitful and harmonious. This is especially important in helping us to see heaven as our continuing service to the king, not passivity or inactivity.

4. CONCLUSION

So, here in this world what can we expect to experience? Verse 22 tells us something of the pains of childbirth. But such pains are experienced because new life is coming, and therefore 'we ourselves have the firstfruits of the Spirit' (23), the beginning of the gospel blessings. We wait eagerly for the full fruits of the Spirit, for the completion of the gospel blessings in glory, when we shall be fully adopted as children into the family, and our bodies will be redeemed.

This is the hope we are saved in, so don't give it up. Don't say, 'Well, I can't believe it because I can't see it.' It would not be hope then, would it? That is what Paul says at the end of verse 24, 'Who hopes for what he already has?' We hope for what we do not yet have (25) and we wait for it patiently. So there are two sorts of waiting – the waiting eagerly, and the waiting patiently, and they go hand in hand. The Holy Spirit is given to us now so that we can express that eager, patient waiting, along with our longing and our groaning. He is within us to interpret our desires as we pray, and to grant us access to the Father, in confidence that the will of God is being worked out in our lives.

It is well worth working through this passage and thinking how it relates to our daily lives. We are people of hope, whose focus is Jesus. We are united to him now and will be united to him forever, in eternity. Our present experience is hope and faith, issuing in love. The practical implications are, 'Keep holding on! It is right that you don't have it all yet.' Such a longing is not a mark that you are not a keen Christian, or that you have not truly trusted Christ. This is normal to Christian life in this world. Nor is there some wonderful experience that will lift you up to another superior level of experience. Keep persevering, keep trusting, keep believing this Christ and keep soldiering on in this world. It will have frustrations; but we hope for what we do not yet have. This is the sure and certain hope of the unchanging promises of God.

2

The Coming of the Lord

There have been many attempts to sum up the message of the Bible in a small compass. A passing generation was reared in Sunday School on a song which said

> God has given us a book full of stories,
> Which he made for his people of old,
> It begins with a tale of a garden,
> And ends with a city of gold.

And in a way that does sum up the Bible, from Eden to the new Eden, from Paradise lost to Paradise restored, from the fall to the restoration.

Some scholars try to focus the message of the Bible on the character of God. After all, he is the prime mover in all its stories, so 'God is the hero of all biblical narratives' (Gordon Fee and Douglas Stewart in 'How To Read the Bible For All Its Worth'). We might say it is a book about 'The God who ...', and then fill in the blanks. We could say it is about the God who saves, the God who rescues. We could say it is about the God who makes and keeps his promises, the covenant-faithful God. We could say it is about the God who *is*, because his name is 'I am who I am', which means that he is eternally unchanging, the same present-tense God, for ever.

1. THE GOD WHO IS COMING

I want to suggest, however, that the Bible is also about the God who comes and that this is a further way of understanding its message, from Genesis to Revelation. Is it not striking that in the Garden of Eden, after man's disobedience, when man is hiding from God, it is God who comes to search out human beings. 'Adam, where are you?' (Gen 3:9)? And Adam is pulled out from behind the trees to face up to what has happened. Here is a God who comes, who does not allow the situation merely to carry on, but who actively intervenes.

Similarly, in the parable in which Jesus describes himself as the good shepherd who lays down his life for the sheep (John 10:11), the whole activity of the shepherd in going in search for the lost sheep signifies the God who comes into the world, in order to rescue us, when we are totally unable to save ourselves (Luke 15:1-7). Time and again, he promises to come in various ways. In the Old Testament, God promises to come through the prophetic ministry, 'I will raise up for them a prophet... I will put my words in his mouth, and he will tell them everything I command him' (Deut. 18:18). In Psalm 110:4, he promises to send an eternal priest in the order of Melchizedek. God is going to come as priest to atone for the sins of his people. And, in the famous passage in Zechariah 9, 'See, your king comes to you, righteous and having salvation, gentle and riding on a donkey' (9), God foretells that he will come as king to deliver his people.

God will come as the *prophet* to declare his authoritative word, he will come as the *priest* to atone for the sins of his people, and he will come to proclaim peace to the nations as the *king* whose rule will extend from sea to sea. This whole strand of promise about Messiah is interwoven through the Old Testament as it progressively unfolds. The king coming to the throne of David is the universal, eternal ruler in God's world, as is summed up in the great title, Immanuel, 'God with us'. The God who is coming is the God who has come.

Rescuer and ruler

When we reach the New Testament, we find that two particular titles – Jesus, the rescuer, and Immanuel, God with us – are placed together in the narrative of Matthew 1, to make it clear that God the ruler, who comes to his people and lives with them, is the one who is also the rescuer of his people. We often talk about Jesus as Saviour and Lord, rescuer and ruler. What we need to remember is that he can only be the rescuer *because* he is the ruler. He cannot be the Saviour unless he is the Lord; but it is precisely because he is Lord that he can and does rescue. The two titles always belong together. God comes as ruler, and when he comes, he rescues in two respects – firstly, *from* his righteous wrath and then *into* relationship with him.

The fulfilment of God's plan

Once we begin to think about the Bible like this, we see that the second coming of Jesus is not some obscure doctrine that is tacked on towards the end of the New Testament. The idea of Jesus Christ's return is not a slightly bizarre, eccentric view of later biblical revelation – it is actually the focal point of all God's purposes. The whole Bible points towards the coming of God: initially, in the coming of Jesus in his incarnation, to accomplish his great work of salvation in the cross and the resurrection. At that point, the New Testament says, the kingdom is inaugurated, the last days begin, and they will only end when he comes again. So everything points towards that final coming.

The return of Jesus Christ in power and in glory is the focus of God's plan and purpose in time, as he brings this world's history to its conclusion, and then on into eternity. So the New Testament encourages us to believe that the countdown has already started. It started on the day of resurrection, and the clock has been ticking ever since, which is why the church always lives in the last days. Here, in the first years of the twenty-first century, we are still in the last days, waiting expectantly and eagerly for that great event to which God is bringing the whole of earth's long history.

There could hardly be a more radical or controversial way of looking at human life in the world from the secular viewpoint. The Bible's view is that history is not cyclical; the human race is not on an endless, repetitive journey. History is linear, progressing towards a clear and definitive end. But the significant factor is this, that as we travel along that linear progression, from Genesis 1 to Revelation 22, we travel with our backs to the engine. We cannot see clearly ahead as to what is coming next, but we can see where we have been and we do know from God's word where we are going. In the Christian life, we can look back on what God has already done and how his promises have been wonderfully fulfilled, knowing that we are 'en route', that we are going to get to heaven in the end, although we do not see the immediate future.

We do not know what is going to happen in the rest of today, let alone the rest of our lives. But as we look back and see all that God has already accomplished in our personal experience, and much more importantly in his great purposes for his whole universe, that gives us the confidence to know that the train is travelling in the right direction, that the driver is not going to go through any red signals, and that we will be brought to eternity with him, because the plans and purposes are his and he has the ability to fulfil them.

This is the sure and certain hope that we looked at in Chapter 1. It stands against all the false hopes of presumption which are the human substitute for biblical hope. But it also stands against all the despair of our world, which is the human expression of our estrangement from God. We live with a firm and secure hope, which focuses on Jesus and which serves as the anchor of our souls (Heb. 6:19). If we put together the ideas of the God who is coming and its focus on Jesus, we see that the return of Christ is the central future reality, which should govern our lives in this world, in the present. We need now to look in more detail at what the New Testament already teaches us about this 'momentous event'.

2. THE TERMINOLOGY OF HIS COMING

In 2 Thessalonians, we find three words used for this future event of the coming of the Lord Jesus. If we can rightly understand the vocabulary here, it will help us with our understanding of the great event itself. Paul writes:-

> The lawless one will be revealed, whom the
> Lord Jesus will overthrow with the breath of
> his mouth and destroy by the splendour of his
> coming (2 Thess. 2:8).

i. A royal arrival

The word translated as 'coming' is the Greek word *parousia*, which carried the original meaning of a royal visit. It was used in secular Greek to signal the arrival of the king or the emperor, in all his authority, to execute his judgments and exercise his rule among his people. This shows us the first meaning of what Jesus is going to come to do. He comes as the king to destroy his enemies – notice verse 8 says that he will overthrow the antichrist with the breath of his mouth – and he will rule his whole creation as the sovereign and lord that he truly and rightly is.

ii. A glory revealed

At this royal arrival, his presence will be manifested in 'the *splendour* of his coming'. That is the second word that is used about the second coming, the word *epiphaneia*, which means an epiphany, or manifestation. So, we have a royal king who is coming to rule, and when he comes to reign, the outshining manifestation of his true glory will be revealed for everyone to see. You could say that when the Queen comes to visit a hospital or a school, her very presence is the revelation of herself and all she stands for. As she steps out of the car, all eyes are on her, and that is the culminating splendour of her coming, the manifestation of her regal office. So when Jesus comes, it will be the outshining of the hidden glory of God that will be revealed, as he takes up his authority to reign.

iii. A reality unveiled

The third word is *apocalypsis*, our word apocalypse, which means an unveiling, and this term we find in the first chapter of 2 Thessalonians:

> This will happen when the Lord Jesus is revealed from heaven in blazing fire with his powerful angels. He will punish those who do not know God and do not obey the gospel of our Lord Jesus (2 Thess. 1:7-8).

There will be a great unveiling, or drawing back of the curtain, showing what was always there but what was not disclosed until this point. At the coming of Jesus, his unveiling will bring relief to his people, to 'you who are troubled, and to us as well' (7), but it will also bring judgment to his enemies, 'He will punish those who ... do not obey the gospel of our Lord Jesus' (8).

Let us bring these three ideas together. Jesus' return is going to be a royal arrival in which the king appears and declares his authority. This will be the manifestation of his splendour, as his glory will be revealed in ways that we find it hard to imagine. It will be the unveiling, or the drawing back of the curtain, in which the reality of Christ's rule will be seen, as he delivers the people he has come to save, and judges his enemies. That is the great event to which we are moving.

3. THE CHARACTERISTICS OF HIS COMING

There are five characteristics of Christ's coming in Matthew 24, which are perhaps familiar to us, but none the less important to highlight. This is the teaching of Jesus himself about his return.

> The sun will be darkened, and the moon will not give its light ... At that time the sign of the Son of Man will appear in the sky... They will see the Son of Man coming on the clouds of the sky, with power and great glory (Matt. 24: 29-30).

i. A personal coming

The first thing we learn about the coming of Jesus is that it is *personal.* When Jesus ascended into heaven, the angels said to the watching disciples, 'Why are you staring into heaven? This same Jesus, who has gone from you into heaven, will come again in the same manner' (Acts 1:11). There will be no change of identity. The Jesus who comes will be recognisably the same Jesus who ascended. In Matthew 24, it is the 'Son of Man' (an Old Testament term for the one who would be given authority and power over God's everlasting kingdom (Dan. 7:13-14), and in the gospels the title that Jesus chose to use about himself) who will come back with personal authority to his world.

ii. A physical coming

Derived from the personal nature of the return, is the fact that it is *physical*. Christ went in bodily form and he will return in the same manner, emphasising the eternal nature of the resurrection body. There is nothing here about a spiritual or mystical return of Jesus. He comes in a glorified physical body. Heaven, too, is a location, not a state of mind, but a place where resurrected physical bodies will be worshipping and serving God in the new environment which is his new creation. We will look at this in a later chapter.

iii. A visible coming

Again, derivative of the previous characteristic, Christ's return will be *visible*. 'Every eye will see him' (Rev. 1:7). This is the answer to the Jehovah's Witnesses who say he returned invisibly in 1914 or any other claim that Christ is secretly present in the world today. There is no incognito return of Jesus; we will all see him.

iv. A sudden coming

Fourthly, it is a *sudden* return. That is to say it will happen, as Paul says, like the coming of a thief in the night, and Jesus is of course the source of that imagery:

> No-one knows about that day or hour,
> not even the angels in heaven, nor the
> Son, but only the Father. As it was in the

> days of Noah, so it will be at the coming of the Son of Man. For in the days before the flood, people were eating and drinking, marrying and giving in marriage, up to the day Noah entered the ark; and they knew nothing about what would happen until the flood came and took them all away. That is how it will be at the coming of the Son of Man (Matt. 24:36-39).

So it will be a sudden appearance. As far as the world is concerned, its inhabitants do not know what is going to happen. Even to his followers, Jesus says,

> 'Therefore keep watch, because you do not know on what day your Lord will come ... you also must be ready, because the Son of Man will come at an hour when you do not expect him (Matt. 24:42-44).

We cannot predict the timing, but we do know it is going to happen and we must be ready for him.

v. A triumphant coming

Fifthly, it is a *triumphant* return. That is to say, he will come again not with his self-emptying purpose, as he did at the incarnation, not as an ordinary human presence, but as the powerful Son of Man, 'coming on the clouds of the sky, with power and great glory' (Matt. 24:30). The coming of Jesus will be the climax of the ages, the fulfilment of God's purpose, his triumphant appearance. The unseen present reality of his sovereign rule will then be made visible everywhere and for ever.

That is why we know that anyone who claims to be Jesus coming back, in anything other than that context, is a liar. When I was assistant to Leith Samuel at Above Bar Church in Southampton, a man came up to us after the service one evening and said, 'I am the Lord Jesus and I have come to my church'. As quick as a flash Leith Samuel said, 'May I see your hands please?' So the man held out his hands, and Leith asked, 'If you are the Lord Jesus, where are the marks of the nails?' The man was down the steps and gone! If that was the Lord Jesus, there would be the mark of the nails in his hands. For it is this same Jesus who will return – personally, physically, visibly, suddenly and triumphantly.

Christ is present in his world now, but his glory is concealed. When he returns, the splendour of his nature and the inescapability of his kingly authority will illuminate the whole created order and reveal its true condition.

4. THE SIGNS OF HIS COMING

Of course what everybody wants to know, as the disciples asked Jesus, is, 'What are the signs of your coming?' (Matt. 24:3). In answer to that question, Jesus gives a number of signs, and it is worthwhile and instructive to examine them in order that we might be ready for his coming and properly prepared to meet him.

One of the most important things to realise about Matthew 24 is that the disciples begin by making a big mistake. At the end of Matthew 23, Jesus has finally pronounced his judgment on Jerusalem in sorrow and in great anguish of heart. He has longed to gather to himself the old Israel, represented by Jerusalem and its temple, but they have rejected him. So right at the end of his ministry, immediately before he goes to the cross, he says to the Jews, 'Look, your house is left to you desolate. For I tell you,

you will not see me again until you say, "Blessed is he who comes in the name of the Lord" (Matt. 23:38). He then walks out of the temple with his disciples, who call his attention to the splendid buildings, the 'house' of the Jews that Jesus has just referred to. It is almost impossible for them to believe that this magnificent temple – reconstructed through the ministries of Haggai and Ezra, and improved hugely by Herod – is going to be destroyed. So he says to them, 'Do you see all these things? ...I tell you the truth, not one stone here will be left on another; every one will be thrown down' (Matt. 24:2). That is a devastating thing for them to hear – that the building at the heart of Judaism is going to be destroyed.

But their mistake is in verse 3: 'As Jesus was sitting on the Mount of Olives, the disciples came to him privately. "Tell us," they said, "when will this happen, and what will be the sign of your coming and of the end of the age?" In other words, they think that the destruction of the temple will be at the same time as Jesus' return. If the temple is going to be destroyed that must be, for them, the end of everything, the Day of the Lord, Judgment Day. If the temple is to go, that must be when the eternal kingdom comes and the Messiah is enthroned as sovereign over all the world – so, please tell us the signs.

In his answer, Jesus distinctly separates the two events from one another. The clear break between verses 28 and 29 shows he is answering their enquiry as two questions and not as one. Some of the signs he describes had to be fulfilled before the temple was destroyed in AD 70, and some await their fulfilment before Jesus returns, at the end.

In this chapter, verses 15 to 20 refer to events which happened in Jerusalem when the Roman armies invaded, under Titus, and began to destroy the city and the temple. Jesus predicts the sign of an 'abomination that causes desolation' standing in the holy place (Matt. 24:15). This is probably the Roman banners and regalia being moved into the temple as they took over, claiming that it belonged to the God Caesar, rather than the God Yahweh. It is a very specific sign, referring to the events predicted in those verses, when the people would 'flee to the mountains' (16). Those events were fulfilled in the destruction of the temple in AD 70, when Jerusalem was besieged, the people were scattered across the face of the earth, and from that time until the mid-twentieth century there was no nation state of Israel established in the land.

i. Ongoing signs

There are other events which refer clearly to the coming of Jesus at the end of time. For example, in verse 14, 'this gospel of the kingdom will be preached in the whole world as a testimony to all nations, and then the end will come.' This is not just the end of the temple, but the end of human history. The destruction of Jerusalem is one of the signs, or one of the events, that had to happen before Christ's return, but the calling of the Gentiles and the preaching of the gospel in the whole world, constitute ongoing signs of God's grace in reaching out to men and women throughout the period of the church's existence, preparing us for his coming.

There is another sign:

> For then there will be great distress, unequalled from the beginning of the world until now – and never to be equalled again. If those days had not been cut short, no-one would survive, but for the sake of the elect those days will be shortened. At that time if anyone says to you, 'Look, here is the Christ!' or, 'There he is!' do not believe it. For false Christs and false

> prophets will appear and perform great signs
> and miracles to deceive even the elect – if that
> were possible (Matt. 24:21-24).

Verse 21 still seems to be describing the Jerusalem destruction, but then the time span lengthens out. Both at the time of the fall of Jerusalem and, we know historically now, down the centuries since, people will come claiming to be Christ returning, or that they know when Christ is going to return. They will claim to have his authority, either to be Jesus or to be one of his forerunners, because they will perform great signs and miracles. But the Bible never encourages us to think that signs and miracles in themselves are a manifestation of God, knowing that the devil can perform all sorts of very impressive supernatural signs to delude and to deceive. 2 Thess. 2:9-10 elaborates this point.

Jesus is saying that there will be false prophets and false Christs who will lead many astray, and that they might deceive even the elect if God permitted it. His point seems to be that such deceit is not possible, because God keeps his own people if they are trusting in him. However, the deluders are so impressive that if God were not keeping them, even God's people would be deceived. So we are warned not to believe them, because as we already know, Christ's coming will be immeasurably greater than any of these deceptions.

> If anyone tells you, 'There he is, out in the
> desert,' do not go out; or, 'Here he is, in the
> inner rooms,' do not believe it. For as the
> lightning comes from the east and flashes to
> the west, so will be the coming of the Son of
> Man (Matt. 24:26).

ii. **The beginning of birth pains**

Jesus is telling the disciples in Matthew 24, 'Don't be surprised when all these things are happening', and he has already given them a whole list of things that are going to happen:

> You will hear of wars and rumours of wars, but see to it that you are not alarmed. Such things must happen, but the end is still to come. Nation will rise against nation, and kingdom against kingdom. There will be famines and earthquakes in various places. All these are the beginning of birth-pains (Matt. 24:6-8).

So when people remark that wars are increasing in the world, and famines and earthquakes seem to be multiplying, should we think we are at the very last stage of those last days? There is no automatic reason to believe because of those signs that we are. Jesus says they are the beginning of birth-pains, and they have been going on all the way through the church's history for two thousand years. He is describing common events by which we should not be thrown into panic or fear.

Similarly, regarding the persecution of Christians, he says:

> You will be handed over to be persecuted and put to death, and you will be hated by all nations because of me. At that time many will turn away from the faith and will betray and hate each other, and many false prophets will appear and deceive many people. Because of the increase of wickedness, the love of most will grow cold (Matt. 24:9).

Again, we see that happening throughout human history. It may well be that this will happen in an intensified form immediately before Jesus returns, but it is not something that is unique to that period. Persecution, people falling away, heresy in the church, and the love of many growing cold for the love of sin, all of these are events which go on throughout the millennia. They are all reminders that Christ is coming, but they are not immediate signs of the event.

iii. The long haul

Jesus is preparing his disciples for a long haul. Towards the end of Matthew 24, he indicates that it is going to be a long time before he comes back, through his story about the servant who is instructed to provide for his master's household. The servant says, "My master is staying away a long time," and he then begins to beat his fellow-servants and to eat and drink with drunkards' (48-49). When the master comes, of course, he verbally cuts the servant to pieces. But Jesus is preparing the church for a long period of waiting. This verse also contradicts the common assumption that he expected that he would come back very quickly and that he was therefore limited in his awareness, as a fallible human being.

These are the signs of his coming and they are meant to remind us of its certainty and to prepare us to be ready to meet him.

5. THE MANNER OF HIS COMING

One problem area concerns the manner of Christ's coming. The second half of Matthew 24 speaks about his return at the end of history. We have moved now beyond the destruction of Jerusalem and we are clearly facing the end of time as we know it: 'And he will send his angels with a loud trumpet call, and they will gather his elect from the four winds, from one end of the heavens to the other' (31). When Jesus comes, he comes for his saints; but what does this mean in terms of the manner of his coming?

> For in the days before the flood, people were eating and drinking, marrying and giving in marriage . . . That is how it will be at the coming of the Son of Man. Two men will be in the field; one will be taken and the other left. Two women will be grinding with a hand mill; one will be taken and the other left (Matt. 24:38-41).

Does this mean that when Jesus returns there will be what is sometimes called the 'secret rapture'? This teaches that the Christians will be mysteriously taken out of the world, into the presence of Christ, and the rest will be left. Since this introduces the whole disputed area of millennial views and expectations about the coming of the Lord Jesus, this is probably a good place to stop and examine some of the issues involved.

The Millennium

The thousand-year period known as the millennium is explicitly mentioned in only one place in the New Testament, in Rev. 20:1-6.

> And I saw an angel coming down out of heaven having the key to the Abyss and holding in his hand a great chain. He seized the dragon, that ancient serpent, who is the devil, or Satan, and bound him for a thousand years. He threw him into the Abyss, and locked and sealed it over him, to keep him from deceiving the nations any more until the thousand years were ended. After that, he must be set free for a short time (1-3).

The period of the devil's incarceration establishes Christ's total supremacy over all the hostile forces of evil and prefigures the ultimate judgment of Satan, when he is 'thrown into the lake of burning sulphur, to be tormented day and night, for ever and ever' (10). Clearly, in the context of the book, this is designed to be a great encouragement to the suffering church, not only to persevere in her witness but also to look forward to the reward which will be hers in the final conquest of all evil. The millennium has a second function, in that it is designated as the time when Christian martyrs will reign with Christ. John continues:

> I saw thrones on which were seated those who had been given authority to judge. And I saw the souls of those who had been beheaded because of their testimony for Jesus and because of the word of God.... They came to life and reigned with Christ for a thousand years....This is the first resurrection. Blessed and holy are those who have part in the first resurrection. The second death has no power over them, but they will be priests of God and of Christ and will reign with him for a thousand years (4-6).

One significant factor is that there is no direct connection of the millennium to the second coming of Christ, within the text. Nor is the thousand years synonymous with the eternal kingdom, since it is of finite duration, and events like the resurrection of the 'rest of the dead' (5), the final judgment and the punishment of Satan which all follow the millennium in chapter 20 precede the revelation of the new heavens and the new earth in chapter 21. Some scholars see implicit references to this intermediate period of Christ's rule in 1 Cor. 15:25 and 2 Pet. 3:8, while others claim the latter reference is an echo of Ps. 90:4, rather than a reference to Christ's rule.

B J Dodd has a helpful article in *The Dictionary of the New Testament and Its Later Developments* (eds. R P Martin and P M Davids, IVP 1997), in which he identifies three main phases in the history of interpretation of the millennium. From the fourth to the eighteenth centuries, most exegetes espoused an 'allegorical or spiritual interpretation' of the millennium. After this, there was a move away from 'creating a fully consistent eschatological scheme' towards regarding the book as an 'apocalyptic mosaic', while more recently still the emphasis has become 'discerning the theological freight of the text' (*op. cit.* p740).

In current evangelical circles interpretation largely falls into one of three groups, each of which we will examine briefly.

Pre-millennialism

Essentially, this view takes the thousand years as a literal period of time, which will be triggered by the return of the Lord Jesus Christ, when the dead will be raised and the living church 'will be caught up together with them in the clouds to meet the Lord in the air' (1 Thess. 4:17). This coming, for his saints, will precede the millennial reign, and is usually connected with Jesus' own teaching about the suddenness of the coming, separating Christians from unbelievers. 'Two men will be in the field; one will be taken and the other left. Two women will be grinding with a hand mill; one will be taken and the other left' (Matt. 24:40-41). Hence pre-millennialism has developed the idea of the 'secret rapture', a concept popularised in recent best-selling Christian fiction in the USA and exemplified in Hal Lindsey's blockbuster *The Late Great Planet Earth* (Zondervan, 1971). Vividly, he imagines what effect the removal of all the Christians from planet earth might have on those who remain, as in this fascinating example.

> It was the last quarter of the championship game and the other side was ahead. Our boys had the ball. We made a touchdown and tied it up. The crowd went crazy. Only one minute to go and they fumbled. Our quarterback recovered. He was about a yard from the goal when zap! No more quarterback, completely gone, just like that.

Such popularisation of pre-millennial views may sell well, but it also complicates the picture by reference to sometimes speculative detail which then becomes the source of internal disagreement. Historic pre-millennialism holds that after the events of 1 Thess. 4:13-17, Christians will rule with Christ on earth. The antichrist will be destroyed (2 Thess. 2:8), the vast majority of the Jews then living will be saved (Rom. 11:25-27) and the Lord Jesus will set up his millennial reign, with his resurrected and transformed saints.

This will be an age of great prosperity and fruitfulness, with Satan bound, but it will be followed by his release, his deception of the nations and their gathering to the last great battle. But Satan is destroyed and the last judgment then occurs, with the whole human race resurrected to appear before the great white throne, out of which the eternal destinies of heaven or hell are decreed. and the final state is reached (Rev. 20:11-15; 21:1ff).

The current complications of this view are usually attributed to what is called dispensational pre-millennialism, which emanates from J N Darby (1800-1882), the originator of the Plymouth Brethren, who suggested significant differences from the classic pre-millennialism, which itself dated back to the second century. This is not the place to go into the complex web of theories which have been spun around these issues. Happily, they have never been as divisive among Bible-believing Christians in the

UK as they have sadly become in some sectors of American evangelicalism. The emphasis in this small book is to concentrate on what is clearly taught in the New Testament and to major on what all can agree, though as soon as one says that it quickly becomes clear that one man's confusion is another man's clarity, and vice-versa! However, the main tenets of the dispensationalist view are that all prophecy is to be interpreted literally and that there is a fundamental and absolute distinction between Israel and the church as two separate communities in the two testaments.

There is an excellent, balanced and informative discussion of the issues in Anthony A Hoekema's *The Bible and The Future* (Paternoster 1978), as also in *The Meaning of the Millennium* (ed. Robert G Clouse, IVP USA, 1977), and doubtless elsewhere in more recent treatments, since it continues to be a hotly-debated issue. Perhaps the easiest source of dispensational eschatology is the *New Schofield Bible* published in 1967, which posits seven distinct dispensations in God's dealings with humankind. Defined as a period of time during which man is tested with respect to his obedience to some specific revelation of the will of God, they are identified as innocence, conscience, human government, promise, law, the church and the kingdom (the last being the millennial reign). But the teaching that Israel and the church are mutually exclusive terms, since God has separate purposes for both, seems to me to be the major rock on which this view founders, in the light of clear New Testament teaching and usage. A full and penetrating critique is provided by Hoekema (*op. cit.* pp 194-222).

Post-millennialism

The post-millennialist view sees the return of Christ as coming at the end of a thousand years of prosperity and peace for the church on earth (which some take literally, though many as a symbolic period). The literal view of Christ visibly reigning from an earthly throne is not part of this position. Rather the millennial age will gradually appear as the gospel spreads across the globe. This view flourished after the Reformation in seventeenth and eighteenth century Europe and America, and was used by God as a great motivator towards missionary endeavour.

The end of the eighteenth century and into the nineteenth century saw a tremendous missionary expansion from the churches of Europe across the world. Post-millennialism was foundational to that missionary expansion because the belief was that the church was on the brink of the thousand years in which the gospel was going to spread across the planet. The revivals that were seen in the eighteenth century were regarded as the first ripples towards a tidal wave of global conversions. Indeed, it is wonderful to see the current expansion of the gospel in the southern hemisphere especially, in stark contrast to the apostasy and neo-paganism of western Europe.

In the nineteenth century, with the secular idea of progress and liberalism's identification of the kingdom of God with social reform, some of the drive went out of post-millennialism, and by and large it has declined. This has undoubtedly been hastened by the world wars of the twentieth century and the current threat of terrorism, which seem sometimes to deny the progress once anticipated.

Challenges to this view are mounted on the grounds that Rev. 20:1-6 does not support the notion of a golden age on earth, so much as the heavenly reign of Christ during the era before his coming. Also, many of the prophecies of the golden age referred to seem more naturally to refer to the final state of the redeemed in the heavenly, eternal kingdom. Finally, as indicated above, it is less easy to be enthusiastic about this view in the light of the world's history over the last hundred years. It certainly does not seem that Satan has been 'bound', as yet, in the sense expected.

A-millennialism

The third view is called a-millennialist, which simply means not millennialist. It is a view which interprets the evidence as being that neither of the other views is sustainable with all the biblical references, and that the 'millennium' should be taken as a symbolic period, rather than a literal period of time. As such, it represents the last days, the whole period from the ascension of Christ to his return in power and glory (Acts 1:11). Building on the apostle Paul's teaching to Christians that God raised us up with Christ and seated us with him in the heavenly realms in Christ Jesus (Eph. 2:6), a-millennialists argue that this is what Rev. 20 is referring to, as the reign of Christ with his saints. This victory, achieved fully and finally at the cross of Christ, and vindicated by his glorious resurrection, ascension and session in heaven, establishes his present sovereignty over the whole cosmos and is the guarantee of his return. At that point, the already inaugurated kingdom of heaven will come in its fullness and the final state will begin. The binding of Satan (Rev. 20:1-3) is evidenced, in this present age, as the kingdom of God spreads through the preaching of the gospel to the nations. The return of the Lord Jesus will be one single event, which will be accompanied by the general resurrection of both believers and unbelievers, the final judgment and the ultimate destinies of eternal punishment or everlasting bliss.

B J Dodd highlights the main objection to this view when he identifies its difficulty as 'It must overlook the current experience of evil in the world, which the author of Revelation conveys as due to the evil one's awareness of the shortage of time left to convert and corrupt (Rev. 12:12)' (*op. cit.* p741). But its great advantage is that it takes the context of Revelation 20 seriously within the book as a whole. It is not a coded message about an unknown future. Darby's aphorism that prophecy is history written in advance is always likely to divert the reader into a quest for speculative detail. Revelation was rather written to strengthen churches under serious persecution and suffering, to show that this was no strange thing happening to them, much less evidence that God had deserted them. Instead, they were to know that Christ and his people will prevail over evil, and that irrespective of the present situation they were to remain faithful, even to death, in confident expectation of the crown of life.

A momentous event

Finally, on all views, whether they are post-, pre-, or a-millennialist, the central expectation of the New Testament is of the coming of Jesus Christ as Lord.

He is the centre of our Christian hope. He is the God who is going to come, and – whether he rules before and after his coming, or after his coming in a thousand year reign, or whether that is symbolic of his sovereignty throughout time and eternity – whatever view we embrace, the ultimate reality remains the same. History is moving towards this great climax. It is not cyclical, but linear, progressive towards its inevitable end, when God will reveal himself in great power and glory, in the returning Son.

Jesus will reign from pole to pole, and he will be the king not only over all his people, but over all who have rebelled against him. As his grace will be exhibited in final and full salvation, so his wrath will be exhibited against his enemies in judgment and in condemnation. And we, who love him, will be with Christ for ever!

This is the momentous event to which our world is moving. Is it any wonder, then, that Paul can say, 'encourage each other with these words' (1 Thess. 4:18)?

3

Personal Eschatology

In this chapter we turn to consider how the last things affect each of us as individuals. As Christian believers, what can we know about what is going to happen in our own personal future? We have been looking at the content of our hope as Christians, and how it centres on the victorious return of Jesus Christ, as King of kings and Lord of lords. That will bring about God's final and eternal rule, the end of all sin and evil, and create the ultimate joy of his people which is God dwelling among them. They will be his people, and he will finally and fully be their God.

What stands between us and that great fulfilment is the experience which we call death. That is where we must begin as we look at our personal eschatology.

How does the Bible define death?
If we look at 1 Corinthians 15, which addresses the subject of the resurrection of the body, we read, 'Christ must reign until he has put all his enemies under his feet. The last enemy to be destroyed is death' (26). The Bible very realistically sees death as

the last and, in a sense, the greatest enemy that we human beings face.

When we begin to explore death in the Bible we soon discover that it is firmly connected to sin. Adam and Eve were told by God, in the garden, that they were not to eat of the fruit of the tree of the knowledge of good and evil, because on that day, he said, 'You will surely die' (Gen. 2:16-17). Although we know that they did not physically die on the day that they had eaten of the fruit, nevertheless death became an inevitable reality for them as a result of that disobedience. Although the sentence was not executed immediately, the warrant was signed by their disobedience.

Death is therefore always seen in the Bible as the wage that sin pays (Rom. 6:23). Physical death is a symbol and a symptom of the much deeper reality of the separation of the individual from God, the source of all life, as a result of human sin.

It is into that terrifying reality that the great good news of Jesus' death and resurrection shines as the gospel light for our minds and hearts. For although death is the last great enemy and a great terror, for the Christian the terror has been removed because of the work of Jesus Christ on our behalf. We know that beyond that separation there is a future reality of union with Christ and fellowship with all his people, for ever.

When Bertrand Russell declared from his materialist viewpoint, 'When I die, I rot', what he was saying was true of his physical body, but not true of his soul. The New Testament teaches that beyond the point that we call death – the paradigm of our separation from God, which we all have to face as the reality of our being human – there is another world and other frameworks of reference, which the Bible goes on to reveal to us as a wonderful comfort and encouragement.

The power of Christ's endless life

The reason we know this is that someone has come back from the other world to tell us. The resurrected Lord Jesus, the Christ who has been through death and overcome it by the power of his own vicarious sacrifice, is the one who is our point of reference, in time and space, in history, for life beyond this world. This is not speculative. Jesus Christ physically rose from the dead in order to declare to his people his great victory over sin, death and hell, and the fact that through him there is everlasting life, the life of the world to come. So when we look at Revelation 21:3 which refers to God dwelling among his people, the very next verse says, ' There will be no more death or mourning or crying or pain, for the old order of things has passed away. He who was seated on the throne said, 'I am making everything new!'" The great problem of death is answered therefore by the death and resurrection of Jesus Christ. When we study the teaching of the apostles in Acts, we find that they are constantly preaching Jesus and the resurrection. It is the resurrection of Jesus, the fact that he has conquered the great enemy, that establishes his identity as Lord and Christ.

He is the mighty king of Psalm 16 who will not be allowed to see corruption, whom God will raise into his presence eternally, a theme to which the apostles constantly return. How do we know that Jesus is the Christ? By his resurrection from the dead. How do we know that his work on the cross is sufficient for cleansing us from our sins and making us right with God? By the fact that God has raised him to his right hand, to the position of authority and power.

It is by the resurrection from the dead that Jesus is demonstrated, as Paul says in Romans 1:4, 'to be the son of God with power'. And just as he has been raised in the power of an endless life, so he will raise his people to share that resurrection glory, and to be eternally alive with him in resurrection bodies. Because we are united to him by faith, what happens to Christ will happen to his people.

1. PERSONAL RESURRECTION

The resurrection of the whole person

When we begin to think in these terms, we realise that the soul and the body are regarded as a unity in the Bible. At a funeral service, it is right to recognise that the real person has gone. We are dealing with the earthly cottage in which he or she lived, and whether that body is buried or cremated, what we are doing is acknowledging the departure of the spirit from the body. The unity has been broken by death.

However, the New Testament does not teach that the immortality of the soul is the focus of the hope that Christians enjoy. Such a view owes something to Greek thinking, which spilled over into Western culture and tended to dominate it following the classical enlightenment. It divided the soul from the body, and not just at the point of death. It saw the soul as being superior, a sort of indestructible spiritual substance, the part of our humanity that mattered most. This is represented in a phrase such as, 'You have an immortal soul to save'. The body was inferior, an envelope of clay, in which the pure soul was imprisoned during our earthly lives.

They were right that the soul will continue beyond this world, but the distinctive Christian perspective on this is that the body also matters and that the body will be raised beyond this world in the power of an endless life. It is not the immortality of the soul that we are looking forward to, but the resurrection of the whole person, body and soul, united in God's presence for ever.

Eternal life as the gracious gift of God

We now need to consider what we mean by the concept of immortality. Paul speaks of 'God, the blessed and only Ruler … who alone is immortal' (1 Tim. 6:15-16). The only immortal person is God, but because he is life and is the source of life, he can give immortality. He can give eternal life, as we call it, but it remains his gift and not something which human souls in and of themselves inevitably have. So Calvin says that immortality does not belong by nature to the soul, but is imputed or imparted by God. He is guarding the view that God is sovereign over everything, and that the soul has no independent existence apart from God's sovereign will. Therefore, he is the one who decides what happens to the body and soul beyond this world, because he is the one who created body and soul and who judges each of us by his own infallible criteria and knowledge (Matt. 10:28).

Eternal punishment as a fearful reality

To contemplate the glories of heaven inevitably raises in our minds the issue of what happens to those who reject Christ and the gospel. The doctrine of the eternal punishment of the wicked has been consistently taught throughout church history, at least until the eighteenth century, by all mainstream theologians and confessions. It is true that universalism, the belief that all human beings will be saved in the end, can be traced back to the early third century, in the teaching of Origen. Moreover, this view has become an orthodoxy among recent more liberal or radical theologians. However, evangelical Christians have always repudiated it.

But another view has gained ground among evangelicals at various times in the history of the church and again in recent years. This position is often called annihilationism or conditional immortality. It focuses upon what the destruction of the wicked actually means and concludes either that the wicked are deprived of their God-given immortality because of their sinful rebellion and so will be annihilated, or that immortality is a gift of God, which is conditional upon faith in Christ, and so will never be given to unbelievers. The origins of this view can be traced back to the fourth century, and today both Jehovah's Witnesses and Seventh-day Adventists teach a version of it, though the latter affirm that there will be a period of punishment preceding the annihilation, as do most evangelicals who adopt this position.

Many of us can empathise with this view from an emotional standpoint. Eternal punishment is a dreadful and horrifying thing to think about, but that does not mean to say that the Bible does not teach it. We dare not build our theology on our emotional reactions, but only on what God clearly teaches in his Word. So let us remind ourselves of the Bible's view of death. Scripture says that it is appointed to man once to die and after that the judgment (Heb. 9:27). Death works no moral transformation in us. Therefore when those who are separated from God by their rebellion and their refusal of his love and mercy face that God from whom they have run away and rebelled against, there is nothing in the Bible to indicate that God will provide some second chance.

It is also important for us to see that destruction, which is the Bible's word for what happens to such people, is not necessarily the equivalent of annihilation. Jesus speaks of a continuing sense of God's judgment and alienation from him. For example, in Matthew 25 he affirms, 'on the last day he will say to those who are his enemies, depart from me you who are cursed, into the eternal fire prepared for the devil and his angels ... then they will go away to eternal punishment but the righteous to eternal life' (41, 46). That is the most horrifying outcome to face, but these are the words of the Lord Jesus Christ himself. He teaches us these things in order to warn us of the realities of eternal separation from God and punishment, banished from his presence. He never teaches that this is for a period of time to be followed by annihilation, but rather that it is to be the continuing experience of those who have rebelled against him. He speaks of a fire that is not quenched. If eternal life, salvation and redemption presuppose an act of God which brings to Christians consequences they are to enjoy unendingly, then eternal punishment must also logically be of unending duration. In this debate we must take seriously the words which the Lord Jesus himself speaks.

It is a concept which is hard for us to grasp, because we inevitably feel extreme unease and grief about it (and should do), but it is designed in the Bible not only to encourage us to turn to God, in daily repentance and faith, but to motivate us to share the good news of his rescue with those who have not yet understood it or accepted it. It is significant that Jesus talks more about the reality of hell than anybody else in Scripture, partly because he knows that reality much more clearly than anyone else, and partly because in his love and his mercy he longs to bar the way to it by calling all who will listen to him to repent. When we repent, in effect, we are saying, 'I know that is where I should be, under God's wrath, and under his condemnation for eternity, in hell, but through the work of Jesus on the cross, he has made it possible for me justly to be forgiven, and I want to put my faith in him to do that.' Then through that faith – which God himself grants us as we listen to his word, understand and believe it – we are united to the Christ who has overcome the power of sin, who has conquered death and delivered his people from hell. All these benefits become ours as we put our faith in him.

2. PRESENT WITH CHRIST

So what is the Christian's experience, then, at the point that we call death? Again, these are mysteries, and it is temptingly easy, but probably not very wise, to be dogmatic beyond what the Bible clearly teaches us. The way in which the New Testament characteristically talks about it is that death is the immediate entrance into a closer communion with Christ:

> For to me, to live is Christ and to die is gain. If I am to go on living in the body, this will mean fruitful labour for me. Yet what shall I choose? I do not know! I am torn between the two: I desire to depart and be with Christ, which is better by far; but it is more necessary for you that I remain in the body (Phil. 1:21-24).

Departing to be with Christ

For Paul, death would be even better than life because it would take him into the presence of Christ in a way that we cannot experience in this world. How many of us contemporary Christians would dare to stand up and affirm a similar view? Yet we all ought to be challenged by it. We are so often exclusively pre-occupied with life in this world that all our concerns come to focus on what our future here will be. That is not automatically wrong in itself, because God gives us an appetite for life in his world, but the startling claim Paul makes is that it is actually better by far to be 'with Christ'.

The point of view which assumes that death is the worst thing that could possibly happen to us, as Christians, is strenuously denied by Paul. He says that ultimately it is the best thing that can happen to us, because we go to be with Christ. How much we find that hard to take indicates how rooted in this world we are! Look how Paul describes it:

> Therefore we are always confident and know that as long as we are at home in the body we

are away from the Lord. We live by faith, not by sight. We are confident, I say, and would prefer to be away from the body and at home with the Lord. So we make it our goal to please him, whether we are at home in the body or away from it. For we must all appear before the judgment seat of Christ (2 Cor. 5:6-10).

Paul is not saying that Christians should exemplify some sort of morbid death wish. But as we look at the inevitability of death – as George Bernard Shaw said, 'Death is the ultimate statistic: one in one dies' – unless we face up to that reality and live our lives now in accordance with its inevitability, we shall always find that death is a terror to us. What Jesus has done is to draw the sting of death, to take the terror out of it.

No balanced Christian is looking forward to dying in the sense of saying, 'I want to be out of this world', and none of us is looking forward to the process of dying, which may be painful, because we do not know how it will happen. Naturally, we are apprehensive about it. Death *is* the great enemy, the last enemy. But, as Christians, we must introduce into that natural human reaction the certain knowledge of what Jesus has accomplished for us. Then we begin to recognise the truth of what Paul is saying, that when we are at home in the body we are away from the Lord, and that when we are away from the body, this mortal life, we will be *at home with* the Lord. That is the great hope, and personal expectation, of every believer.

No separation

We have this same confidence from the lips of the Lord Jesus himself. Remember how in his last words on the cross, he says to the dying thief, 'Today you will be with me in Paradise' (Luke

23:43). Notice the phrase *with me*: heaven is being with Jesus. Where Jesus is, heaven is. Where his people join with him, that is what heaven is all about. The picture in Revelation is of his people around his throne rejoicing in his presence, in the great victory that he has won for them. So the moment we call death, in biblical understanding, is the moment in which a person to whom God has given eternal life through the gospel, is transferred into the very presence of Christ himself. Our assurance is further strengthened when we realise that in the gospel the verdict of the last day has already been pronounced. We are not guilty (Rom. 8:1). We have passed from death to life (John 5:24).

This teaching totally denies any concept of *purgatory*, paying for one's sins or undergoing a cleansing process, after death, to prepare for heaven. Such ideas entirely lack any scriptural support. Similarly, the idea of *soul sleep*, that death renders the soul 'unconscious' until its reunification with the resurrection body, seems quite contrary to the sense of Scripture. The Bible talks about believers falling asleep, but this is simply another term for death. It is the body which 'sleeps', not the soul.

Those who die in the faith of Christ will consciously be in the presence of God, like those souls of the departed in Revelation, crying out,

> How long, Sovereign Lord, holy and true, until
> you judge the inhabitants of the earth and
> avenge our blood? (Rev. 6:10)

Surely, Paul would not say it is better by far to depart and be with Christ, if the soul was going into cold storage. Rather, he affirms that we go directly into the presence of the Lord Jesus, to be with him in eternity, for ever. What we are waiting for is the resurrection of the body and the life of the world to come.

3. PERMANENT FUTURE

Jesus teaches that he is the one who grants us immortality, brings us into his presence at death and, who will raise us in resurrection bodies on the last day (John 6:40, 11:25-26, 14:1-3). Moreover, he is the prototype of this. In the resurrection of Jesus, the life of the world to come has burst into our world of time and space. The Kingdom of heaven touches our physical, temporal existence on planet earth wherever Christ's life is manifested. The frontier post between these two worlds exists wherever Christians live in this world as citizens of heaven, sharing the life of God through the indwelling of the Holy Spirit. But our real home and our true fulfilment awaits the life of the world to come; not as disembodied spirits, but as fully integrated and complete body and soul persons.

The resurrection of the body

We live our lives as Christians on earth at the overlap of the ages, of this world and the world to come. At the last day, those who belong to Christ, who have already been made new within, through the new birth, will be given a resurrection body, perfectly suited to life in the new environment of the eternal kingdom. It will be related to our present body, but in the way in which a flower is related to a seed. There will be discernible continuity, but also amazing transformation. In the life of the world to come, each one will be a unique reflection and expression of Christ, in a unique resurrection body. That resurrection body will reflect his glory, but it will also be continuous with our personhood in this world (Phil. 3:20-21, Col. 3:3-4).

When Christ came to the disciples in his resurrection body, he was recognisable as the same Jesus they had known throughout his earthly ministry. When they were fishing on the lake and the figure on the beach called out to them, John said to Peter, 'It is the Lord' (John 21:7). To the disciples in the upper room on Easter evening, 'he showed them his hands and side' (John 20:20). To unbelieving Thomas he said,

> Put your finger here; see my hands. Reach out
> your hand and put it into my side. Stop doubting
> and believe (John 20:27).

So the risen Lord Jesus is continuous with the Jesus who was crucified. The resurrection body of Christ is identifiable as the same body that was killed on the cross.

When Paul says in Philippians 3: 21 that our lowly bodies will be transformed to be like his glorious body, he does not mean that we will all physically look like Jesus, but that Jesus' resurrection is the pattern for our resurrection. As there was continuity between the earthly Jesus and the risen Lord, there will be continuity between our earthly bodies now and our risen bodies at the last day. That is why recognition will be possible in heaven, because we will be our own unique selves in Christ, yet without any of the weaknesses and imperfections which so mar and spoil our lives in this world.

He will deal with all our weaknesses and develop us into the maturity which God originally intended us to experience and enjoy, the complete person in Christ that he designed us to be, body, soul and spirit, for eternity. Each whole person will be raised in a resurrection body, patterned on Christ's glorious resurrection body, to live in the eternal kingdom of the new heavens and the new earth, as a perfect reflection of the Saviour who loved us and gave himself for us.

What we are redeemed for

Of course, this is mind blowing and we need to give time in meditation just to allow it all to sink in. This is where Christians are going, and this is what we are going to be, because it is for this that God's great redemption plan was activated. It is immeasurably wonderful that we are going to be fully *like* Jesus (1 John 3:1-2). We are also going to be *with* Jesus, where all the things that hinder us, depress us and frustrate us now will be removed. We are moving towards the experience of being with Christ, which is better by far.

The new body will be the perfect vehicle for us to express the redeeming grace of God. Rather than seeing heaven as sitting on clouds, twanging harps and singing choruses forever, we need to understand that God has limitless gracious purposes for us to fulfil in his new creation. All the unique abilities he has given to us as individuals will be working together with the whole body of Christ, to bring glory to him throughout the new creation for ever and ever. It is mind blowing, but it helps us to begin to grasp something of what the gospel has achieved, so that we start rejoicing now.

So let us not be reductionist. We looked in Chapter 1 at how our hope should animate our evangelism. This is clearly what our non-Christian friends need to hear – where we are going and what is going to happen to us as Christians, what the great hope of salvation is. They may laugh at us and dismiss it as 'pie in the sky', they may turn their backs on God and rebel against him, but we must not do them the disservice of failing to tell them the whole story. The gospel is not just sins forgiven, wonderful though that is, it is far more than that. It is people like us re-made into the likeness of Christ, so that all that God purposed in his first creation will be fulfilled in the new creation, on an unimaginably greater and grander scale.

We must never separate redemption from creation, or think that creation was a work for this world, but redemption is a work for the world to come. No, God takes the creation and renews it. He redeems all that he has made and he will bring it to fulfilment in that new creation – the new heavens and the new earth, in which righteousness dwells (Rom 8:18-25).

Raised to meet Christ

> Brothers, we do not want you to be ignorant about those who fall asleep, or to grieve like the rest of men, who have no hope. We believe that Jesus died and rose again and so we believe that God will bring with Jesus those who have fallen asleep in him. According to the Lord's own word, we tell you that we who are still alive, who are left till the coming of the Lord, will certainly not precede those who have fallen asleep. For the Lord himself will come down from heaven, with a loud command, with the voice of the archangel and with the trumpet call of God, and the dead in Christ will rise first. After that, we who are still alive and are left will be caught up together with them in the clouds to meet the Lord in the air. And so we will be with the Lord for ever. Therefore encourage each other with these words
> (1 Thess. 4:13-18).

This is a key passage. We need to realise that all our hope about our personal future is rooted in what Jesus has already done in the past: 'We believe that Jesus died and rose again and so…' (14). Everything depends on the work of Jesus on the cross and on the resurrection. Because we know that he has died and risen again, we know that those who have fallen asleep in him will also be raised, 'God will bring with Jesus those who have fallen asleep in him'. That is why we do not grieve as those who have no hope. Our expectation is that we shall come with Jesus, if we have died before his return on that great day. And, 'according to the Lord's own word', we who are still alive will certainly not precede those who have fallen asleep. We shall not be at any advantage if we are still living in this world. Our privileges will be the same; our destinies identical.

How the second coming and the great fulfilment will happen, is that the 'Lord himself will come down from heaven, with a loud command, with the voice of the archangel and with the trumpet call of God, and the dead in Christ will rise first' (16). After the dead have risen, those who are alive will be caught up with them to meet the Lord in the air (17), transformed into his likeness in a moment, in the twinkling of an eye. So, in a mighty act of God's creation, which heralds the new heavens and the new earth, all God's people will be united together with the Lord.

At that point, as the eternal kingdom begins, and the new environment is created, the church will be one, totally united from every nation, tribe and time in history, complete in the presence of the sovereign king himself, and lifted up to be with him for ever. That is the encouragement, as we put strength into one another, which this teaching is designed to give us. It is a wonderful expectation of the future so, however we may try to comfort people in this world, however we ourselves are comforted in times of bereavement and loss, and whatever residual questions we may have, it is vital never to give up this hope which we do know about, for the sake of what we do not yet know. We must hold on to what God has clearly revealed, that this is where he is going to take us and that not one of his believing people will be lost, so that we can look forward to that great and glorious day, with confidence and joy.

For those who are not yet his people, Scripture reminds us that '*now* is the day of salvation' (2 Cor. 6:2). Those who put their faith in him and trust him now will certainly share this glorious future as their own, rather than the dreadful separation from God which must come to those who are his enemies. If we are his people, then we must be animated by this hope, not only in our evangelism, but in our quest for holiness, and in all the details of our lifestyle in this world. We are citizens of another country – a heavenly one – and like Abraham, our great example of faith, we are 'looking forward to the city with foundations, whose architect and builder is God' (Heb. 11:10).

4

The Way the World Ends

What are the cosmic implications of Jesus coming back and winding up human history? T S Eliot summed up two possible alternatives very neatly in his famous lines: 'This is the way the world ends / Not with a bang, but a whimper'. But are either of these the way you think the world will end?

1. CONFRONTING OUR MATERIALIST CULTURE

If scientific materialism ever seriously considers the end of planet earth, its view of how it might occur probably oscillates between the two options, the bang and the whimper. On the one hand, when people do think about the end of the world, it is usually in terms of horrific possibilities, such as nuclear warfare wiping out the whole of the planet. They recognise that the endgame scenario, beloved by the movie makers, could be triggered at any time. Or, if it might not be nuclear conflict, what about those films which envisage meteorites hitting the earth, or aliens invading from outer space?

Or perhaps it won't be a bang, but a whimper? A gradual fade-out, with the earth getting either colder or hotter, according to your theory, until it can no longer sustain life. After all, it is claimed that the history of mankind is just a remarkable accident, on a minor particle of matter, in a vast unfathomable universe. So, the chemical reaction which began the long process by which living things have evolved to their present infinite complexity could, with equal absence of purpose, be reversed or just fade out, and humankind will be gone.

Bertrand Russell popularised this view of the ultimate purposelessness and futility of life in *A Free Man's Worship*.

> Man is the product of causes which had no pre-vision of the end they were achieving. His origin, growth, hopes and fears, loves and beliefs, are but the accidental collocation of atoms. No fire, no heroism can preserve an individual life beyond the grave, the whole temple of man's achievement must inevitably be buried beneath the debris of a universe in ruins.

At first, words like these sound brave and desperately realistic to our culture, because they describe the only freedom left to the atheist, to shake his fist in the face of the God from whom he is running away, and to proclaim that human life is in fact without meaning or any lasting significance. We need a healthy corrective.

i. The Scripture's view: wholesome thinking

> Dear friends, this is now my second letter to you. I have written both of them as reminders to stimulate you to wholesome thinking. I want you to recall the words spoken in the past by the holy prophets and the command given by our Lord and Saviour through your apostles.

First of all, you must understand that in the last days scoffers will come, scoffing and following their own evil desires. They will say, 'Where is this "coming" he promised? Ever since our fathers died, everything goes on as it has since the beginning of creation.' But they deliberately forget that long ago by God's word the heavens existed and the earth was formed out of water and by water. By these waters also the world of that time was deluged and destroyed. By the same word the present heavens and earth are reserved for fire, being kept for the day of judgment and destruction of ungodly men.

But do not forget this one thing, dear friends: With the Lord a day is like a thousand years, and a thousand years are like a day. The Lord is not slow in keeping his promise, as some understand slowness. He is patient with you, not wanting anyone to perish, but everyone to come to repentance.

But the day of the LORD will come like a thief. The heavens will disappear with a roar; the elements will be destroyed by fire, and the earth and everything in it will be laid bare (2 Peter 3:1-10).

This passage takes head-on the reaction of the godless world to the realities which we have been examining in the previous chapters. Its first two verses are easily passed over, but are actually foundational to everything that follows. Peter is saying to his readers that he wants to stimulate them to wholesome thinking, which is always the great goal of apostolic ministry. Our minds need to be shaped by God's revelation in a wholesome way, so that we start to think right. Comparatively little thinking is done among Christians today concerning these issues. Indeed, because there are so many confusions and disagreements, we are tempted to wonder whether it is really worth the effort. Yet to know where the world is going and how it will end can hardly be insignificant!

Verse 2 makes a really important contribution, because it shows us how to foster wholesome thinking about the future, 'I want you to recall the words spoken in the past by the holy prophets and the command given by our Lord and Saviour through your apostles'. Peter is reminding his readers that they need to know God's revelation about his future plans contained in both the Old and the New Testaments, so that on the basis of the divine disclosure they can begin to think realistically about the future.

It is important then that our conclusions are totally shaped by Scripture, while recognising that the Bible does not necessarily tell us everything we would like to know (Deut. 29:29). Sometimes, we will have to acknowledge that we have no clear biblical idea, in answer to a particular question or piece of speculation, not only because we may not understand the Bible well enough, but principally because the Bible does not give us the answer. It can never be a bad thing for a Christian to say, 'The Bible doesn't tell me that'. A much greater danger is to become dogmatic in areas where we are actually most speculative, since this is always likely to cause unhelpful and unnecessary divisions.

It is God's word which teaches us what is going to happen to God's world. That was Bertrand Russell's great mistake. Highly intelligent and able man that he was, he assumed that the world could effectively explain itself without the need for revelation. But the world cannot achieve that end because the world is the expression of the mind of God, its creator, and the mind of

God is only revealed authoritatively in the word of God. Verses 1 and 2 clearly state that if we are going to understand anything, it will be by revelation, as God declares his mind to us, created beings. Moreover, the only way we shall come to understand the future is by paying attention to what God has said in the past, through both the Old Testament prophets and the New Testament apostles, not by reading the newspapers, or listening to the evening news.

ii. The Scoffers' view: deliberate unbelief

Moving to verse 3, we see Peter's concern for his readers to understand that, in the last days, 'scoffers will come scoffing'. He is using a Hebrew way of expressing intensity, by repetition. These proud mockers will do what they are naturally gifted to do, and they will do it intensely. Such scoffing will be based on various kinds of pseudo-intellectual reasons, and will raise all sorts of arguments against God's revealed Word, but their real reason is so that they can follow their own evil desires.

Paul Johnson's book, *The Intellectuals*, focuses its thesis on this very issue. Reviewing a dozen or so great intellectual figures of the last two hundred years, he shows that their godless intellectualism was actually promoted in order for them to have liberty to fulfil their own evil desires. The scoffers scoff because they want to live godless and immoral lives. This will usually be packaged in philosophical concepts and in sophisticated, intellectual language and will almost certainly propound all sorts of destructive theories. Verse 4 gives us examples, 'Where is this "coming"?' Surely you don't still believe in that after two thousand years do you? 'Ever since our fathers died, everything goes on as it has from the beginning of creation.' It sounds so reasonable and contemporary, yet Peter's warning is clear – 'but they deliberately forget'.

What they forget is what God has already said through his prophets and apostles. They forget it deliberately in the sense that they consciously remove God's truth from their minds in order to reject it. It is not that it just slips from their memory, but that they deliberately choose not to incorporate it into their frame of reference. So there will always be conflict between the Christian and the scoffer. The scoffer is always going to come with his own arguments, seeking to reject God's words so that he can follow his own evil desires, but it is only by the Word of God that the world can be understood and that the future will be known. See, for example, the equivalent idea in Heb. 11:3.

In order to make this point, Peter draws the parallel in verses 5-7 between Noah's flood and the coming future judgment. Reminding us that the Word was the means by which the heavens and the earth were formed, he states that it was also the means by which the ancient world, of Noah's time, was deluged and destroyed. God said, 'Let there be light', and there was light. He spoke his word, and the heavens existed, and the earth was formed. But he later spoke a word of judgment predicting that he would flood the earth, and that is what he also did. Furthermore, it is by that same infallible Word of the living God, that 'the present heavens and earth are reserved for fire, being kept for the day of judgment and destruction of ungodly men' (7).

So when a scoffer comes along saying, 'Well it's two thousand years since all this was promised, why hasn't it happened?', we come back to what Jesus himself taught, which we looked at in Chapter 2. Our foundation of confidence about the future lies in the unchanging word of God. When our hearers are browbeaten by those who assert that because it has not yet happened it will not happen, then we need to take them to the next couple of verses, to nerve and strengthen their faith.

iii. The 'slowness' of God

In verse 8, Peter cautions, 'Do not forget this one thing, dear friends: With the Lord a day is like a thousand years, and a thousand years are like a day.' He is affirming that God is not bound by time. What *we* may think is a very long time, is for him like a couple of days. Therefore, looking at it from God's perspective, we recognise that the fact that the end has not yet happened is not that the Lord is slow in keeping his promise, as humans understand slowness. Rather, there is wonderful gospel truth at the heart of this apparent delay. 'He is patient with you, not wanting anyone to perish, but everyone to come to repentance'(9).

When unbelievers scoff at our belief in the Bible's view of the end of all things, we can respond with humble confidence that we do believe it is all going to happen, but that it is wonderful that God has been patient until today, because if Jesus were to have come yesterday, there would be no opportunity today to receive his salvation. Peter's point is that the Lord's 'slowness' is not an indication that he cannot keep his promises. He is neither late, nor negligent; nothing is outside his control. Rather, he is patient, gracious, and forbearing, not wanting anyone to perish, but everyone to come to repentance.

However – and here is the bedrock of apostolic teaching – the day of the Lord will come and it will be like a thief. The apostles had thought at one time that they could know when it would take place. But Jesus taught them that it would be unexpected, that there would be many false prophets and false teachers, by which Satan would try to cut the line of God's truth in any way he could (Mk 13:32-36). Indeed, if he could cut out the second coming then of course there would be no ultimate judgment, and nothing to make us human beings accountable to God. So verse 10a is a very important statement. 'The day of the Lord will come', and at that point the heavens and the earth will disappear.

2. THE DAY OF THE LORD

With that basis then, let us look further at the phrase, 'the day of the Lord', because it is part of the central biblical vocabulary for the way the world ends. It is the classic biblical terminology for the climactic event to which all human history is inexorably moving.

i. A long foreshadowed day

In chapter 13 of Isaiah, the prophet begins a section of his book consisting of ten chapters, full of oracles delivered about and against the nations, speaking about God's judgment inevitably coming on their ungodliness and wickedness. For example, in Isaiah 13:1 we find 'An oracle concerning Babylon'. The historical nation of Babylon is described here, but there seems also to be a wider and more representative meaning. From the tower of Babel in Genesis 11, to the city of Babylon, in the book of Revelation, Babylon is representative of human society geared against God in proud independence, of man in all his arrogance fighting God's sovereignty. What will the outcome of such rebellion prove to be?

> Wail, for the day of the Lord is near; it will come like destruction from the Almighty. Because of this, all hands will go limp, every man's heart will melt. Terror will seize them, pain and anguish will grip them; they will writhe like a woman in labour. They will look aghast at each other, their faces aflame (Is. 13:6-8).

That is precisely what happened to Babylon, when it fell to the Persians and experienced a great massacre of its citizens. But look at the following verses and notice the vocabulary:

> See, the day of the Lord is coming – a cruel day, with wrath and fierce anger – to make the land desolate and destroy the sinners within it. The stars of heaven and their constellations will not show their light. The rising sun will be darkened and the moon will not give its light. *I will punish the world for its evil*, the wicked for their sins. I will put an end to the arrogance of the haughty and will humble the pride of the ruthless. I will make men scarcer than pure gold, more rare than the gold of Ophir. Therefore I will make the heavens tremble; and the earth will shake from its place at the wrath of the LORD Almighty, in the day of his burning anger (Is. 13:9-13).

That is what the day of the Lord is about. What we learn from these two juxtaposed paragraphs is that the judgment on Babylon was significantly a prototype of the great last judgment of the world.

All the judgments of the Old Testament, though real and actual in themselves, are also prototypical. They foreshadow the great end judgment, called the day of Lord, which will bring the wrath of God against all the rebellion and wickedness of men. We need to recognise that the prophecies of the Old Testament have multiple fulfilments. At one level, they have fulfilments within the period of the Old Testament, but at their second level, they come to fulfilment in Christ. Further, most of them have total fulfilments only in eternity, because the gospel is an eternal revelation of God, and the work of Jesus has eternal repercussions. So we should not be surprised to find that what is said in the Old Testament relates to the New, and on beyond the New into the eternal kingdom.

ii. The last day

All the way through the New Testament we find reference to the fact that we are living at the end of the ages – 'on us the *fulfilment* of the ages has come' (1 Cor. 10:11), 'Jesus appeared at the *end* of the ages to do away with sin' (Heb. 9:26), 'Dear children, this is the *last* hour' (1 John 2:18). Frequently the apostles are in fact saying, 'Almost everything in God's great plan has already happened. The only event that now remains is the last climactic intervention, when the drama of earth's history finishes as the author walks on to the stage at the end of the play and the story is wound up.' And on that day, *his* day, the creator exerts his authority over all history in judgment, and over all the future in sovereign power.

iii. The day of rescue

We have seen that the day of the Lord is a day when God comes both to judge and to rescue his people from that judgment. So on that day, when the heavens tremble and the earth shakes and the wrath of the Lord is revealed in burning anger, Jesus also rescues us from that judgment. Then we shall know what a great salvation we have and what a wonderful work God has done for us. The day of the Lord, which Peter is talking about, the day of fire and burning anger, the end of the age, is the great certainty to which both the Old Testament prophets (e.g. Isaiah 2:12-22) and the New Testament apostles (e.g. 1 Thess. 5:1-9) constantly direct us.

iv. The day of judgment

As we have already had cause to note, Revelation 20 is a key chapter for understanding this great event:

> Then I saw a great white throne and him who
> was seated on it. Earth and sky fled from his

presence, and there was no place for them. And I saw the dead, great and small, standing before the throne, and books were opened. Another book was opened, which is the book of life. The dead were judged according to what they had done as recorded in the books. The sea gave up the dead that were in it, and death and Hades gave up the dead that were in them, and each person was judged according to what he had done (Rev. 20:11-13).

This day of the Lord is the day of his judgment. It is a scene of almost unimaginable awe and majesty, with the great throne occupied by the Lord God. The whole creation is fleeing from his face, but every human being, 'great and small', is summoned to the presence of God, before whom they stand, and the books are opened.

From the context, we can assume that the books are the books of human lives, the books that record the deeds of everyone who is standing before the throne: 'The dead were judged according to what they had done as recorded in the books' (12). Everybody is included: those who have been drowned, those who are dead, those in Hades, the abode of the dead, all of these stand before the throne of God. And everybody is judged on the same basis, 'according to what he had done.' So the judgment is made on the basis of works, of what we have done.

It is very clear that none of us will have the right of access into God's heavenly presence on the basis of what we have done, because the Bible tells us all the way through, 'there is none righteous, no not one', and all our righteous acts are as filthy rags in God's sight (Is. 64:6, Rom. 3:10-18). But the key issue is that when the books are opened and everyone is found guilty, there is another book opened, 'which is the book of life…If anyone's name was not found written in the book of life, he was thrown into the lake of fire' (12 & 15). So, on that judgment day, the only escape from punishment will be that one's name is discovered in the book of life. It is one of the clearest statements in the whole of the Bible about the fact that if we rely on our works we are condemned. Rather, we are to be totally dependent on God's gracious gift of life through our names being written in his book, by virtue of the work of the Lord Jesus on our behalf.

Everything that is opposed to God's perfect reign of truth and love, righteousness and peace must now be destroyed. Therefore, death, Hades and the devil himself are thrown into the lake of fire, because God is demonstrating that there is ultimately only one prevailing power, in the whole created universe. He is the one who determines the future of everything: for he is the creator and he is the judge.

v. The day of reckoning

We have seen that the last day which will surely come is the day of the Lord, a day of judgment, on which everybody is found guilty. However, some are taken into life rather than into punishment, because their names are found in God's book. But also, at the end, there is an assessment of those whose names are written in the book of life. Paul tells the Corinthian believers, 'We shall all stand before the judgment seat of Christ' (2 Cor. 5:10).

By this he seems to mean something rather different from the great white throne of Revelation 20:11 before which the whole human race is judged. The apostle is teaching us that our lives will be assessed by the Lord Jesus, so that each one may receive what is due to him for what he has done during this life. This is not a judgment to heaven or hell, so much as a judgment of our faithfulness and service. In 1 Corinthians, Paul talks about this reality in terms of Christian ministry, stating that at the last day God's fire will bring to light the quality of the work which each person has built, and if what he has built survives, he will receive his reward (1 Cor. 3: 12-15).

The nature of rewards

At this point it may be helpful to stop and look more closely at the main points of Scripture's teaching about rewards, since it is so little heard today, but is clearly designed to strengthen our hope and motivate our obedience in service. The positive hope of enjoying God's rewards and the negative threat of losing them are certainly intended to be powerful persuaders for our present activities in this world to be prioritised, according to the future. The theological reason for this is the close connection between faith and work, the latter being the evidence of the former. 'As the body without the spirit is dead, so faith without deeds is dead' (Jas. 2:26). Jesus himself taught the same connection, in the closing paragraph of the Sermon on the Mount, where the wise man who builds his house upon the rock 'hears these words of mine and puts them into practice' (Matt. 7:24). Famously too, in the parable of the sheep and the goats (Matt. 25:31-46), the separation between the two classes, with their totally opposite destinies, does not depend upon an investigation into the good works the 'sheep' have done in sufficient measure to earn God's acceptance. The decision is made by the King alone (33), but the parable goes on to reveal its reasons. It is not that the ministries of mercy in which they have been involved – feeding the hungry, entertaining the stranger, clothing the naked or visiting the sick and the prisoner – have procured their place in God's eternal kingdom. The 'sheep' actually do not recognise when they did these things (37), so there was clearly no intention of earning merit by their works. They were simply expressing their love and devotion to the king, by ministering to others described by Jesus as 'these *brothers* of mine' (40). Their works of mercy and love were the demonstration of the reality of the saving faith in Christ as Lord, which they professed. As Calvin once expressed it, 'It is faith alone which justifies, and yet the faith which justifies is not alone' (quoted by A Hoekema, *op cit*, p261).

But if it is true that salvation is only and always by God's grace alone, through faith in Christ alone, it is also the case that at least two New Testament passages indicate a variation of reward among true believers. The most famous is the parable Jesus tells, in Luke 19:12-19, about the nobleman who goes to another country 'to have himself appointed king and then to return' (12). His servants are given different quantities of minas, ten, five and one, which they are to put to work for him against his return. The first two servants double the ten and five mina investments and receive charge of ten and five cities, as a reward, but the one-mina servant, who has done nothing with the deposit, loses it all. It seems, therefore, that faithful service of the Lord Jesus in this life will produce equivalent rewards in the life to come, perhaps mainly in terms of increased responsibility. That seems to be the idea also in the Pauline passage, 1 Cor 3:10-15, where the quality of Christian service is exposed by the fire of God, on the last day, and where what is built survives that searching judgment, because of its quality, this will be rewarded. It is important to recognise this as an assessment of *service*, not a requirement of works for justification. The reward is never conceived as being earned or deserved, but always the gift of God's grace.

This is a powerful reminder that the gospel is not simply that we are forgiven, so that what we do with our lives subsequently does not matter, or that whether we are faithful or faithless is irrelevant. Instead, there is to be a sifting or testing of Christians, which functions as God's assessment, at the end of our lives. What we need to grasp and remember is that any rewards we receive are not earned by our merit, but are given graciously and freely by God. The rewards are not so much an incentive for us to follow in God's ways, rather, Paul is saying, that everything which is done for the glory of God, faithfully in his service, is known by God and treasured by him, and will have eternal repercussions. What we do in this world does have influence on life in the world to come.

Jesus is not saying that our heavenly reward consists of putting our feet up and having plenty of money in the heavenly coffers, but that we will have the wonderful fulfilment of serving him even more in the life to come. Those responsibilities are themselves part of the great joy of heaven.

3. BEYOND THAT DAY:
ENDLESS DAY & ENDLESS NIGHT

The wonderful reality of heaven

This, then, is the day of the Lord, the great coming day on which he sorts the sheep from the goats, and when he declares those whose names are written in his book, the day in which his people rejoice in their great salvation. This clearly sends us in two different directions, to think about heaven and to think about hell, the endless realities which Scripture clearly teach lie beyond 'that' great day. We need to look at both briefly, here.

John 14:1-6 is a familiar passage, often used at funeral services, because it is such a clear text about the meaning of heaven. Jesus said,

> Do not let your hearts be troubled. Trust in God; trust also in me. In my Father's house are

many rooms; if it were not so, I would have told you. I am going there to prepare a place for you. And if I go and prepare a place for you, I will come back and take you to be with me that you also may be where I am. You know the way to the place where I am going . . . I am the way . . .

The picture language must not be taken over-literally. Jesus is not going to build a motel for us! He is not going to get the room ready, make up the bed and put our name on the door. What he is saying is, 'My going is the way in which the place is being prepared for you. I am going, through the cross and the resurrection, to the ascension in glory. That is what prepares the way in heaven for you.' It is his *going* that prepares the place. By his death and resurrection he has become the way, so that through trusting in him who died in our place on the cross, all those incriminating records in the book of our deeds can be blotted out by his precious blood and our names transferred from the book of guilty rebels to the book of life. Such fulfilment will be heaven.

However, it is equally clear that heaven is a *place*. Children sing that zippy little song, 'Heaven is a wonderful place, full of glory and grace'. It is a place which the death of Jesus opens up for his people, not an amorphous state of mind. Jesus is very concrete about it. The ascension and his return 'in like manner' are so important precisely because they are physical, bodily events. And what is the nature of that place? It is wonderfully described in verse 3: 'that you also may be where I am'. The greatest certainty we have about heaven is that we will be present there with the Lord, because where Jesus is, there is heaven.

You might like to look at these references for further study on the reality of the heavenly experience: Revelation 7:15-17;

11:16-18; 12:10-12. In chapter 6 we shall attempt to explore more of what we can know about the realities of heaven, to put the biblical flesh on the skeletal concept.

The dreadful reality of hell

If there is a heaven to be gained, then there is a hell to be shunned. The word that is usually translated 'hell' comes from the Aramaic word *gehenna*, which occurs in some of the English translations of the Synoptic gospels. The Valley of Hinon, Gehenna, was the place where the rubbish from Jerusalem was put outside the city. It was a continuously-burning rubbish dump. Jesus used the picture of gehenna as a visual image of the awful reality of an eternity cast out from the presence of God.

Hell is not the same as Hades. Hades is another Greek word signifying the abode of the dead. So in New Testament thinking, the departed believer goes to be with Christ immediately, but the soul of the unbeliever is kept in Hades, the abode of the dead, until the last judgment, 'The sea gave up the dead that were in it, and death and Hades gave up the dead that were in them, and each person was judged according to what he had done' (Rev. 20:13). Ultimately, heaven and hell belong to the period following the last judgment, when the new heavens and the new earth constitute what we call 'heaven', and being cast into the lake of fire constitutes what we call 'hell'.

Beyond Hades there is the experience of hell, the unquenchable fire that the Bible speaks about, that eternal restlessness and lostness. I think it is quite helpful to think of heaven in terms of perfect *rest*, which is not doing nothing for ever and ever, because the Bible says 'his people will serve him' (Rev. 22: 3), but to think of hell as total *restlessness*. Remember how Isaiah repeats in his prophecy, 'There is no peace for the wicked says my God': there is no rest (Is. 48:22; 57:21). And in

Revelation 14:11 we are told, 'There is no rest day or night for those who worship the beast and his image, or for anyone who receives the mark of his name'. There is no rest, and the smoke of their torment rises for ever and ever.

Likewise, when people say that they will not mind going to hell because all their friends will be there, they could not be more tragically mistaken. There will be no friends in hell; the very concept will no longer exist. Everything that derives from God in terms of goodness in this world will no longer be there, which is why hell is such a terrifying prospect. It is a dreadful thing, to be lost, to be outside of God's kingdom, to be in what Jesus described as outer darkness.

I remember the Australian evangelist, John Chapman, recalling how when he spoke at one university mission, a young lady came up to him at the end of an address in which he had been talking about hell, and accused him of trying to frighten her into the kingdom of heaven. She objected strongly to what she identified as emotional blackmail. His characteristic reply was to ask her why she felt so threatened. If what he had said was true, then he had told her in Christian love, so that she might be rescued. If, however, it was *not* true, why was she feeling fearful and threatened? She felt threatened because she instinctively knew that it was true, as every atheist knows instinctively the God that he, or she, is running away from (Rom. 1: 19-20).

We must not be apologetic about this. I think it was Wesley who said that if we preach hell, we should do so with the tears streaming from our eyes. That is so right. You cannot preach hell with an unbroken heart. But we must preach hell, if ever we are to preach heaven. One of the great tragedies of our contemporary context is that so much gospel preaching is evacuated of hell, and therefore ultimately evacuated of heaven. All that is left is that Jesus will pep you up and give you a good life here that will be a little bit better than if you did not accept him. What a travesty of the gospel that is! We need to preach the reality of Scripture with all the sensitivity, conviction and faithfulness God can give us. This is the way the world ends.

4. OUR DEATH IS IN HIS HANDS

There is one final piece of assurance to add to our review of these momentous issues. It is found in Revelation 1, where the Lord Jesus is revealed in all his splendour and glory. He declares, 'I am the Living One; I was dead, and behold I am alive for ever and ever! And I hold the keys of death and Hades' (Rev. 1: 17-18). Jesus holds the keys of death, because he has conquered our last and greatest enemy. This means that your death, and mine, is not in anyone else's hands but those of the Lord Jesus. Isn't that a wonderful thing to know? Each Christian is immortal until their work is done in this world. In that sense, you cannot die before God's time, and when it is God's time, then and only then will it happen. He holds the keys of death, and when it happens, we will be present with the Lord. He also holds the keys of Hades, that is to say that he is in control of all departed spirits, of all those who have lived this life and died, whether they are believers or not. He is in sovereign control of all, because he is the Lord of the universe, 'the First and the Last, the Living One', who was dead himself and who is now alive for ever and ever.

There is great certainty here which should motivate us to go out in compassion and mercy to those who as yet do not believe. The end of the world will bring about the righting of wrongs, the swallowing up of death in life everlasting. As Jesus says, 'All who are in their graves will hear the voice of the Son of Man and come out. Those who have done good will rise to live, and those who have done evil will rise to be condemned' (John 5:28).

Or, as Paul says before Felix, 'There will be a resurrection of both the righteous and the wicked' (Acts 24:15). These things are confirmed, therefore, not only by the Old Testament prophets, but by the words of the Lord himself and by the words of his apostles.

For the Christian, there is certain hope: 'Whoever hears my word and believes him who sent me *has* eternal life and will not be condemned; he has crossed over from death to life' (John 5:24). And, 'Everyone who looks to the Son and believes in him shall have eternal life, and I will raise him up at the last day' (John 6:40). If Christ will do that for us in this world, by cleansing us and renewing us, what will he give us in the world that is yet to come? (Rom. 8:31-32).

5

The Shape of Things to Come

Then I saw a new heaven and a new earth, for
the first heaven and the first earth had passed
away, and there was no longer any sea. I saw
the Holy City, the new Jerusalem, coming down
out of heaven from God, prepared as a bride
beautifully dressed for her husband. And I
heard a loud voice from the throne saying, 'Now
the dwelling of God is with men, and he will
live with them. They will be his people, and
God himself will be with them and be their
God. He will wipe every tear from their eyes.
There will be no more death or mourning or
crying or pain, for the old order of things has
passed away.'

He who was seated on the throne said, 'I am
making everything new!' Then he said, 'Write this
down, for these words are trustworthy and true.'

He said to me: 'It is done. I am the Alpha
and the Omega, the Beginning and the End.

> To him who is thirsty I will give to drink without
> cost from the spring of the water of life. He
> who overcomes will inherit all this, and I will
> be his God and he will be my son. But the
> cowardly, the unbelieving, the vile, the
> murderers, the sexually immoral, those who
> practise magic arts, the idolaters and all liars –
> their place will be in the fiery lake of burning
> sulphur. This is the second death' (Rev. 21:1-8).

It is a bulwark conviction of reformed and biblical theology that the Bible is one book, one story. Or, to use the contemporary terminology, one 'meta-narrative', which overarches the whole of our individual human experience, and the whole experience of the human race from beginning to end. It is, of course, profoundly counter-cultural to say this, because people today do not believe that there could be any ultimate truth that makes sense of it all. That is perhaps the essence of post-modernism. To say that history has a meaning, let alone a destination, is literally incredible to most of our contemporaries.

But as Christian people, who take the Bible seriously, in its total revelation, we do believe that Scripture provides the explanation of everything which God has been doing along the timeline from Creation to the great event described above, the coming of the new Creation, the new Jerusalem. So it is not surprising that the last two chapters of the last book of the Bible focus on the end of that story.

1. A NEW CITY

The dominant idea in Revelation 21 and 22 is the image of the new Jerusalem as 'the Holy City'. In that one powerful symbol of the new Jerusalem coming down from heaven the final vision of the Revelation is captured for us. It is the arrival of this city on the scene of John's vision which inaugurates the new creation and the full manifestation of all of God's eternal purposes.

Normally, we tend to sum this up in the one word 'heaven', but we have seen that heaven is a word with a wide variety of reference points. For example, the kingdom of the heavens is the eternal kingdom which broke into time and space history when Jesus came into the world in his incarnation and was manifested when he began his earthly ministry. On the other hand, we talk about believers having gone to 'heaven', when we mean they have gone to be with Christ, in his immediate presence.

Here in Revelation 21-22, it has the extended meaning of *the new heavens and the new earth*, which constitute the eternal context, in which our everlasting life is to be lived out. And, as with the other familiar terminology we have been trying to understand, the 'new heavens and new earth' is one of those well-known terms which trips off our tongue easily enough, but is not quite so easy to pin down. The purpose of this chapter is to come to a clearer definition of what is, in fact, the shape of things to come.

i. We shall live in a new environment

In the reality of the final judgment, which we looked at in Revelation 20, the 'old order' was removed, and in Revelation 21:1 we see 'a new heaven and a new earth'. If we are talking about heaven, how can there be both a new heaven and a new earth?

We need to recognise that the term in the Bible 'heaven and earth' is simply a way of expressing the totality of our environment. We live on planet earth and above us we see the blue sky which is called the heavens ('The heavens are telling the glory of God', Ps. 19:1). The new heavens are the new surrounding of the new earth, that is the new environment in which God's people are placed. So a new heaven and a new earth simply present a composite term for the eternal environment in which we and all God's redeemed people will live.

ii. We shall know continuity between old and new

We need to bear this idea of our new environment in mind as we look back at 2 Peter 3, which will help us to see a little more clearly the transition at Revelation 21.

> But the day of the Lord will come like a thief. The heavens will disappear with a roar; the elements will be destroyed by fire, and the earth and everything in it will be laid bare. Since everything will be destroyed in this way, what kind of people ought you to be? You ought to live holy and godly lives as you look forward to the day of God and speed its coming. That day will bring about the destruction of the heavens by fire, and the elements will melt in the heat. But in keeping with his promise we are looking forward to a new heaven and a new earth, the home of righteousness (2 Pet. 3:10-13).

At first sight, it seems as though a total obliteration is predicted when this passage declares that 'everything will be *destroyed*' (11). But it is important to bear in mind that in this very context the same word is also used about the world of Noah's day: 'By these waters also the world of that time was deluged and *destroyed*' (2 Pet. 3:6). Clearly, that world 'ended' in terms of the destruction of the people living in it, as it was submerged under water. But planet earth was not finally destroyed by the flood so that it did not exist any longer. It was a different world beyond the flood and yet it was the same earth.

So, we need to be careful before we take destruction necessarily to mean total obliteration, with 'heaven' having no connection with what went before. That is not the way Peter is using the word in verse 6, and therefore in verse 11 we must keep in mind that there is at least some continuum from the old order to the new. When Revelation 21:1 says, 'I saw a new heaven and a new earth, for the first heaven and the first earth had passed away', it is a new *environment*, but it is not something which is so totally removed from the old, that it has no connection to it. John could obviously recognise this new environment as being 'heavens and earth', not something *completely* alien to his experience.

The people whom God has redeemed will be transferred from one environment to the other, just as the character which we have developed during our lives in this world will remain with us. Although it is impossible for us to begin to appreciate the full glories of the heavenly kingdom in this world, yet the Bible does not hesitate to use imagery of our lives here to depict the coming, eternal realities. So, in Revelation 21 and 22 the idea of the city, the new Jerusalem, with its constant supplies of light, water, food and community point to a continuum between our experience of life now and the life of the world to come. The same idea surely lies behind Revelation 21:24, 'The nations will walk by its light, and the kings of the earth will bring their splendour into it.' If the beauties and treasures of this world are wonderful, then we can be sure that the joys and fulfilment of heaven will far outshine them. Moreover, all that we have offered as service to our Lord in our earthly pilgrimage, all that is of lasting value and pleasing to him will be preserved to his glory and for our reward (1 Cor. 3:12-15). Just as the resurrection body started as a seed which flowers into its fullness beyond this world, in a similar way the new heavens and the new earth are the flowering of God's gracious and wonderful purposes for creation.

iii. We shall live as the bride of Christ

Perhaps we should be less concerned with the geography of the Holy City, and more concerned with its theology. Returning to Revelation 21, the next thing to strike us is that the vision of the city is compared with the appearance of a bride. As the new Jerusalem comes down from heaven, *prepared* by God, to be the environment in which his people will live forever, John's comparison is with a bride on her wedding day, beautifully dressed for her husband,

> One of the seven angels . . . said to me, 'Come,
> I will show you the bride, the wife of the Lamb.'
> And he carried me away in the Spirit to a
> mountain great and high, and showed me the
> Holy City (Rev. 21:9-10).

This is not only a visual image of comparison, since the Holy City is not merely a physical environment. It expresses an eternal reality because, of course, the bride of Christ is the church. It is the community of redeemed people who make the City and who are at the very heart of God's eternal purposes. This God-given environment, described in very concrete terms, is animated and comes to life with the people who live within it.

The most significant difference about the City is that now at last 'the dwelling of God is with men' (3). God comes to his redeemed people as Father, Son and Holy Spirit, interacting in love and harmony, in the three persons of the Godhead, dynamically forever. And when God dwells among his people in that way, they will be relating to one another also in love and harmony forever. Because his perfection is reflected in the people he has redeemed, the City is Christ-shaped. It is God's creation, his gracious provision, since he made us for relationships with himself and with each other. That love, reflecting the very heart of God himself, will be the hallmark of heaven.

iv. We shall live in the full light of God

As John sees the shape of things to come in the new Jerusalem, a key phrase is, 'It shone with the glory of God' (Rev. 21:11). All that follows is an expression of this dominant idea of the inner nature of God's character shining out in the manifestation of his glory. Clearly, the concept of shining and brilliance links God's glory with light. In this, John echoes the prologue of his gospel, where he says of Jesus coming into the world, 'The light shines in the darkness, but the darkness has not *understood* it' (John 1:5). This verb like several others in John has a double meaning. Some English translations opt for 'overcoming' rather than understanding. But the most helpful rendering I have found is in a commentary on John's Gospel by JN Sanders and BA Mastin (Hendricksen, 1968) where they translate the clause 'but the darkness has not *mastered* it'. This seems to me to be the best English equivalent. The darkness cannot master the light since it can neither understand it, nor can it overcome it. Not only does the darkness of rebellion and sin fail to comprehend God's self-revelation, but also it cannot do anything to quench or extinguish that light.

v. We shall radiate the full light of God

The glorified city shines with the glory of the Lord, which means that the same light also shines from the people of God. In his gospel, John writes, 'The Word became flesh and made his dwelling among us. We have seen his glory, the glory of the One and Only, who came from the Father, full of grace and truth' (John 1:14). As those who are in Christ, we reflect his glory now, in a measure, and we will reflect it in all its fullness in the eternal city.

This theme of the church as the source of God's reflected light in the world is a favourite one in John's writings. Right at the beginning of the book of Revelation, John hears a loud voice calling out and telling him to write on a scroll what he sees. He turns round to see that it is none other than the risen Lord Jesus speaking:

> And when I turned I saw seven golden lampstands, and among the lampstands was someone 'like a son of man', dressed in a robe reaching down to his feet and with a golden sash round his chest. His head and hair were white like wool, as white as snow, and his eyes were like blazing fire. His feet were like bronze glowing in a furnace ... His face was like the sun shining in all its brilliance (Rev. 1:12-16).

It is a dominating vision of amazing light, so strong that he almost could not look at it. But where is the exalted glory of Christ discovered? 'Among the lampstands' (13). The very last phrase of chapter 1 holds the interpretation, 'the seven lampstands are the seven churches' (1:20). So the glory of the risen Christ is seen among the churches, among his people. That is where God has now determined that his glory will dwell, as we are called to be his light-bearers.

The glory of Christ is already seen now in some measure in the church which functions as his light in this dark world. So Jesus says to his followers, 'You are the light of the world' (Matt. 5:14). But what is true in a measure now will come to its completion in eternity, when the whole heavenly city shines with the light of the king, as each of us his people is transformed into his likeness, to become a uniquely brilliant expression of the glory of God. Like so many countless billions of light particles shining, each individual, each unique Christian, will reflect the glory of Christ, the brilliance of his person, the splendour of his character. That is the shape of things to come.

vi. We shall experience completeness multiplied by infinity

It is not surprising then in Revelation 21, that after John's statement that the city 'shone with the glory of God', everything that follows is perfection. The city is surrounded by a high wall, as Isaiah prophesied, 'You will call your walls Salvation and your gates Praise' (Is. 60:18). The contextual emphasis in Isaiah seems to be on God fulfilling all that he has ever promised in the completeness of his salvation purposes. So God's protecting care, his steadfast love and his dependable character are all symbolised by the strong walls which surround the city of God and guard his people. This is what makes the city of Zion impregnable. God has surrounded her with his salvation, which is dependent on his faithful promises, and therefore could not be more secure.

Perhaps one of the greatest expressions of this in the English language is John Newton's magnificent song of exultation

> Glorious things of thee are spoken
>> Zion, city of our God!
> He whose word cannot be broken
>> Formed thee for his own abode.
> On the Rock of ages founded

What can shake thy sure repose?
With salvation's walls surrounded
Thou may'st smile at all thy foes.'

We need words like these to respond to this vision of glory, not just with a measure of intellectual comprehension but from hearts set on fire with love and praise. If teaching the Christian hope does not produce something of that response in ourselves and in our hearers, the subject matter has penetrated very little beneath the surface of our lives.

Next there are the twelve gates that give access to the four square city:

> It had a great, high wall with twelve gates, and with twelve angels at the gates. On the gates were written the twelve tribes of Israel. There were three gates on the east, three on the north, three on the south and three on the west. The wall of the city had twelve foundations, and on them were the names of the twelve apostles of the Lamb (Rev. 21:12-14).

The symbolism is not too difficult to understand. Listed on the gates and the foundations are the tribes of Israel, from the Old Testament, together with the apostles of the Lamb, from the New Testament, both numbering twelve, the number of completion, because this represents the fulfilment of all God's promises to Israel, completed in Christ as those from all nations stream into the Israel of God. The numbers are symbolic and therefore the picture of the four square city, with gates in sets of three on each of the four sides, indicates that from whatever point of the compass any individual may come, access is available for the total number of God's chosen people. Not one is missing from the gathering in the city.

The names of the twelve apostles on the foundations indicate that the city is founded on their apostolic testimony and teaching. They are apostles of the Lamb because their message is all about the Lamb who died and was raised again, centred on the great atoning work of Jesus on the cross. The foundation of the city is the true gospel of Jesus Christ, the Lamb of God, who takes away the sin of the world, faithfully preached by his apostles. This is the both security and the eternal nature of this city.

In verse 15, 'The angel ... had a measuring rod of gold to measure the city ... The city was laid out like a square ...He measured the city with the rod and found it to be 12,000 stadia [1,400 miles] in length, and as wide and high as it is long.' Remembering that this is an apocalyptic book in which the numbers are symbolic, the measurement is simply saying, 'It is so big that you cannot get your mind around it.' It is twelve times one thousand. One thousand is a symbolic number in apocalyptic writing for the incalculable, and twelve, as we have seen, is the symbolic number for completeness. God is telling us that if we multiply completeness by infinity we will have some idea of what this city is like! The symbolism is designed to humble us into amazement and adoration.

Once we begin to think like that and then see that the city is represented as a perfect cube – 1,400 miles up, across, and at every dimension – we begin to realise that we are not just being introduced to a new city, but to a whole new creation. However, the city imagery allows us to hold on to the reality with terms which we can at least *begin* to understand. As we progress, we find descriptions like this:

> The wall was made of jasper, and the city of pure gold, as pure as glass. The foundations of the city walls were decorated with every kind

> of precious stone...The twelve gates were
> twelve pearls ...The great street of the city was
> of pure gold, like transparent glass
> (Rev. 21:18-21).

Of course, this is nothing like a photograph! If we try to think in those terms we are bound to get it wrong. What the writer is saying in effect is that we should hold a picture, in our mind's eye, of magnificence, of unimaginable quality, splendour, wealth and value, and then realise that, to an infinite degree, this is what God will produce in this new creation. Our finite human minds, tied to this world, are stretched by language which we can understand, and yet cannot comprehend. God's city is so far beyond us, so unimaginable in its glory, splendour and triumph.

But they are all images which indicate reality. We must not just write them off as mere picture language, as though no concrete reality was intended. Nor, at the other extreme, must we become too literalistic, saying for example, 'If there is no night there how am I to get any sleep? Won't I be terribly tired?!' Take the picture language and see how it transcends your mind and recognise that it is meant to do so. But you cannot miss the great central concerns: at the heart of the city is the Lamb as the temple, the Lamb as the light and it is the Lamb's Book of Life which alone guarantees entry into the city. This is the first strand – the new city. We, his people in Christ, are that city, reflecting the glory of God, now in a measure, then in its fullness.

2. A NEW INTIMACY

This leads us to explore the second idea about the shape of things to come, which I want to call the new intimacy.

i. **God will dwell among us forever**

This is the way in which John wants us to think about the reality which lies ahead. This city is the dwelling of the king of kings, indicating that the Lord God is dwelling with his people, that is to say he dwells *within* them, as well as *among* them. If they are the city, then the implication is that every individual member is filled with the life of God.

> And I heard a loud voice from the throne saying, 'Now the dwelling of God is with men, and he will live with them. They will be his people, and God himself will be with them and be their God (Rev. 21:3).

The essential hallmark and experience of heaven is God with us. Even more than that, it is God within us. As always, we find the root of this great fulfilment idea back in the Old Testament. In Leviticus 26:11-12 God promises, 'I will put my dwelling place among you, and I will not abhor you. I will walk among you and be your God, and you will be my people.' In the Old Testament this promise that God will pitch his tent among his people is the greatest blessing of the covenant. It was initiated with the Exodus deliverance from Egypt and constituted the great blessing which God guaranteed to Israel if they lived in obedience to him –they could live in unhindered fellowship with this God.

In the first five books of the Bible, especially in Exodus, the big question which continually resurfaces is, 'How can a holy God, dwell among a sinful people?' The short answer to that is the provision of the tabernacle. The 'tent of meeting' was set up in order that acceptable sacrifices might be offered, so that the offences of sinful people might be covered and so that they might continue to live in the presence of God. So Exodus 25:8

instructs Moses, 'Have them make a sanctuary for me and I will dwell among them.' The purpose of the tabernacle was that God might come down and dwell with his people symbolised by the *shekinah* ('dwelling' is the literal meaning) cloud of glory. The cloud and the fiery pillar provided an external picture of the spiritual reality of God dwelling among his people.

But the extraordinary thing is that when the tabernacle was set up at the end of the book of Exodus, in accordance with all of God's instructions and the cloud of glory came down upon the tent, nobody could enter because the glory of God filled the place. We are being taught this irony that when God comes to dwell with people, his glory is so magnificent that it actually excludes his people from his presence (Exod. 40:34-35). The question remains, therefore, 'How can sinful people ever live in the glory of such a holy God?'

To answer this enigma we must remind ourselves that the Pentateuch is one unit. So the book of Exodus ends with the tabernacle filled with the glory of God and Moses not being able to enter the Tent of Meeting because the cloud of the Lord had settled on it. The next book, Leviticus, begins with God speaking to Moses from the Tent of Meeting, telling him to say to the Israelites, 'When any of you brings an offering to the LORD, bring as your offering an animal from either the herd or the flock' (Lev. 1:2).

How are sinful people to live in the presence of a holy God whose glory is overwhelming, who is like a consuming fire that would destroy them? They are to bring offerings from the flock, in the form of sacrifices. The sacrificial system is necessary because of the glory of God. Indeed, it was the only way that a holy God could live among his sinful people. Only by the blood of sacrifice, offered through priestly intercession, could sinful people ever be acceptable to God. That, of course, is why Jesus is called the Lamb of God who takes away the sins not only of a nation but of the world (John 1:29).

So how will New Testament people dwell in heaven? How can we ever see God's face and dwell in his presence, which is what we are promised in Revelation 22? Only because an offering has been made – a full, perfect, sufficient satisfaction for the sins of the whole world. The Lamb of God has carried away our sins in his own body, on the tree. Everything is brought to perfection in Christ. The theme of the tabernacle and the temple, the place where God's people meet with him, now finds its ultimate fulfilment in the heavenly reality, where they will never be separated from him, where God will reveal himself to and through his people, unhindered, for ever and ever.

ii. We shall see his face

The essence of eternal life is the life of the eternal within each of his people. There is no need of a temple in which to worship God, because the whole city is the temple. We are each one in relationship with God. There is no need of a lamp because the Lamb is the lamp. In Jesus, the light who has shone in the darkness, our lives are continuously illuminated. There is no night there; everything is perfect light.

> They will see his face, and his name will be on their foreheads. There will be no more night. They will not need the light of a lamp or the light of the sun, for the Lord God will give them light (Rev. 22:4-5).

What an amazing promise that is that we shall see his face. How could sinners like us ever see the face of God and live? Nobody in the Old Testament could do that. Here, the people of God are made right with God for ever through the sacrifice of the Lamb, and the Lamb is the fulfilment of all those promises

– the light, the meeting place, the sacrifice. We shall see his face, and seeing his face we shall be like him, reflecting his glory. In the words of Paul, 'We are the temple of the living God.' As God has said, 'I will live with them and walk among them, and I will be their God, and they will be my people' (2 Cor. 6:16).

iii. We shall be like him

This is very thrilling for us even in the present, because the process is already underway. In 2 Corinthians 3:18 we read that, 'We, who with unveiled faces all reflect the Lord's glory, are being transformed into his likeness,' *from one degree of glory to another.* That is to say, what started when we first became Christians, is being developed and processed all the way through our pilgrimage in this world.

We must never undervalue what God is doing now, in transforming us into his likeness. I remember seeing a young Christian with a slogan on his T-shirt, 'Be patient, God hasn't finished with me yet'. That is right; that is the Christian's motto. God has not finished with us yet, because we are growing more and more into the likeness of Jesus, changed from one degree of glory to another, as we trust and obey him. It is by a pale reflection here in this world, but it will be face to face in the world to come. That is where we are going, and that is the shape of things to come. The process is already underway.

So it is not wrong to ask, 'Am I more like the Lord Jesus this year than I was last year?' There ought to be progress. We ought to be able to see one another growing that little bit more like Jesus. We may not be able to see it in ourselves, but as we look for it in others, we most certainly do see it. God will bring this process to fruition. It is not that heaven is all out there, in the future and remote from us now. Rather, what God is doing in us now, he will take right through to the heavenly fulfilment. We are already on the way to glory, and we can rejoice and praise God for that, as we see one another growing in grace and in our knowledge and love of him.

3. A NEW CREATION

The third idea regarding the shape of things to come is new creation.

> He will wipe every tear from their eyes. There
> will be no more death or mourning or crying or
> pain, for the old order of things has passed away
> ... I am making everything new! (Rev. 21:4-5).

We must never forget that redemption is not an end in itself. It is the means to an end, and this movement from creation to the new creation is at the heart of biblical eschatology.

i. God makes his people new

Israel was always aware that her very existence as a people was the product of God's sovereign choice: 'Let us kneel before the LORD our Maker. For he is our God and we are the people of his pasture, the flock under his care' (Ps. 95:6-7). The expression, 'the Lord our Maker' is an Israelite expression, meaning not that he is the creator of all human beings, but that he made Israel his flock, his special possession.

So if the church, now including believers from all the nations, is the true 'Israel of God' (Gal. 6:16), then we too are made by our God. We are given this new identity as the new creation in Christ. We are new creatures, in Christ, the people of his pasture, the flock under his care. What he did for Israel by redeeming them through the Passover lamb, he has done for us through Christ, our Passover lamb, sacrificed in our place (1 Cor. 5:7).

Redemption is necessarily the renewal of God's rule in our lives. Because of the fall we have all become rebels, true sons of Adam and daughters of Eve. We have all lived our lives without reference to God, following our own way. But the Lord has caused to meet on Jesus the iniquity of us all (Is. 53:6). And as Jesus has carried the punishment and penalty of our sin, so now God will redeem us, making us new, and recreating us into the likeness of Christ.

ii. God makes his creation new

In the same way, God also takes his cosmic creation and redeems it, making it the new creation. Just as Adam, God's original creation, was placed in a perfect environment, so Israel, the newly-created people of God, was taken to the land flowing with milk and honey, the focus of God's perfect and total provision. There the temple was eventually built, where God dwelt among his people, where they knew him as their God and worshipped him as their king.

Logically, the community of God's redeemed creation must also have a new environment. When Paul calls the church 'the Israel of God', he is saying that all Christians, all over the world, from every tribe, nation and language, and also throughout history, have been formed into God's new covenant community. God is going to bring them all to a new environment, to a heavenly home.

He is making everything new. That is a profound description, not just of God's activity in and through Jesus Christ, but of his very nature. The essence of God is that he is always creating and always renewing. So the biblical witness that begins in Genesis 1 ends in Revelation 21 with the new creation. The whole story of salvation is contained between these fixed points.

It moves forward all the while by divine intervention, as God is constantly doing new things. He intervenes in Noah's day by providing the ark, so there can be a new world beyond the flood. He intervenes in Moses' day by providing the Passover, so there is a new world of freedom beyond Egypt. He intervenes in the days of the exile by providing Cyrus his shepherd, who allows God's people to return to their land, so that there is a new beginning back in Jerusalem, with Ezra and Nehemiah.

He intervenes supremely in Christ coming into the world as the second man, the last Adam (1 Cor. 15:45 ff). In this role, Jesus not only lived the perfect life that all of us in Adam have failed to live, but he also died the death that we deserved to die, as the atoning sacrifice in our place, and everything is made new as a result.

The blessings of Revelation 21 are the eternal expression of all the foreshadowed blessings promised in the Old Testament. They are wonderful blessings – no more death, no more crying, no more pain, no more night, no more curse – because through his redemptive work, he has made everything new. He has produced the perfect environment for his redeemed people. As Isaac Watts says in one of his hymns, 'In Christ the tribes of Adam boast more blessings than their father lost'. It is not just Eden restored; it is far greater and far more wonderful than that. God is going to recover his original intention – with all its infinity of potential – by redemption through resurrection, so that ultimately nothing will be outside his sovereign rule of his new creation.

iii. God accomplishes all his purposes

We cannot understand redemption properly without seeing it as the accomplishment of God's original creation purposes. When Jesus came, as the king, he came in person to execute his Father's will, and to carry out his good purposes. When he comes again in glory, we will see the completion of it all. The significance of that is that we shall be personally redeemed, into the likeness of Christ. We are going to become everything God originally intended us to be, but which has been so spoiled by our sin and rebellion. That is amazing, but it is on a much bigger scale even than that.

He is going to bring about a whole new cosmos, a whole new environment, a new creation, in which we, as believers in the gospel, are an integral part. The change which the gospel affects in us is the pledge of what will one day transform the whole created order. We do not yet see everything under his feet, but we do see Jesus, crowned with glory and honour, risen, ascended, glorified (Heb. 2:8-9). This Jesus, who is himself the good news, is God's righteousness revealed and made available to us, through faith, as we turn to him and trust him.

Heaven will be living in the context of God's unadulterated righteousness, with nothing to spoil, hinder or harm. All the divisions and barriers caused by sin will be broken down and finally obliterated. All the ethnic, social and cultural divisions will be gone. We shall be 'all one in Christ Jesus' (Gal. 3:28). That *is* the eternal gospel, the eternal righting of all the wrongs. But it is not *just* that. Heaven is the creation of something immeasurably more wonderful than we can ever imagine, as the eternal reality of God dwelling among his people makes everything new.

We need to keep on believing in our redemption within its proper biblical context of eschatology, the creation and the new creation. Christians have the only credible narrative that can make sense of the world. It is a major tragedy when evangelical Christians settle down for a 'me-centred' pietism, rather than seeing this glorious programme of the whole created order. But sadly, our world view is all too often too small, because we are so restricted by our present experience. As redeemed people, we need constantly to call one another to renew our minds, according to God's truth, to a world view that is truly gospel-shaped.

This gospel declares that Jesus Christ is Lord – Lord of everything, Lord of everywhere, Lord for eternity. He reigns for ever and his will shall be done. So, the new creation is not just the consequence of the cross, it is the climax and goal of God's purposes through the cross. What is the shape of things to come? The Lord Jesus – to whom every knee will bow and every tongue confess that he is Lord – as the Almighty sovereign over all creation. And we, who love him now, will reign with him for ever.

6

What Sort of People?

He is the image of the invisible God, the firstborn over all creation. For by him all things were created: things in heaven and on earth, visible and invisible, whether thrones or powers or rulers or authorities; all things were created by him and for him. He is before all things, and in him all things hold together. And he is the head of the body, the church; he is the beginning and the firstborn from among the dead, so that in everything he might have the supremacy. For God was pleased to have all his fulness dwell in him, and through him to reconcile to himself all things, whether things on earth or things in heaven, by making peace through his blood, shed on the cross (Col. 1:15-20).

1. JESUS CHRIST: CREATOR AND FULFILLER OF ALL THINGS

As we begin this last chapter, we need to remind ourselves of our starting-point, which was that the Christian's hope is founded on the person of the Lord Jesus Christ himself. Perhaps the clearest statement of this great truth is to be found in this passage from Colossians, which provides us with so many encouraging reminders about how everything finds its fulfilment in him. The passage is divided into two segments by the repeated term 'firstborn'. In verse 15 we read that Christ is 'the firstborn over all creation', and then in verse 18 that he is 'the firstborn from among the dead'.

Firstborn over all creation

In the first section (15-17) which deals with creation, the Lord Jesus, standing apart from the whole creative sequence as its originator, is revealed to us as the image (*icon*) of the invisible God. Thus he is the exact representation in visible, human form of the nature and character of the invisible God. As human beings, we were originally made sons of Adam, created in the image of God. So, in his humanity the Lord Jesus as the perfect man is the perfect image of the invisible God. In the incarnation, that image of God, so long defiled and spoiled in our fallen human state, suddenly reappears in the perfection of God's Son. The Lord Jesus, as he comes into the world to fulfil his Father's will and to accomplish his great work of salvation, which will lead ultimately to the new heavens and the new earth, reveals all that we, as human beings, were intended to be.

But Jesus is far more than that. Verse 16 shows that he is nothing less than God: 'For by him all things were created: things in heaven and on earth, visible and invisible …all things were created by him and for him.' In Jesus, the embodiment of the divine nature, the rule of God is exercised throughout his creation. Everything was created by him and for him, and everything holds together in him.

It is at this point that the significance of the language about the 'firstborn' becomes clear. The firstborn son inherited everything that the father had provided for him: he was the one to whom the whole estate came. To describe Jesus as the firstborn means not only that in time he pre-exists all created things, but that he is the *inheritor* of all these things. Everything in creation belongs to him. He is prior to it all in time, and sovereign over it all in eternity.

Therefore, the Lord Jesus is the revelation of what the new redeemed humanity will be like in him. As the one who in himself is the perfection of humanity, he will bring every one of his children into that state, each as a unique reflection of his perfection.

All this is operating in the sphere of our present experience, since this creation, our world with all its beauty, and glory and wonder is the revelation of the mind of its creator. He is also the goal to which it is moving and the way by which it coheres and holds together. Christ is the Lord of the cosmos, since the whole creation is for him, by him and in him.

Firstborn from among the dead

In a balancing section, verse 18 proclaims that the Lord Jesus is the head of the new creation, for it states, 'He is the head of the body, the church; he is the beginning and the firstborn from among the dead, so that in everything he might have the supremacy.' The Lord of the universe, the cosmic Christ, is the Lord of the church and the Lord of eternity. He is the beginning and originator of that whole new creation.

'Firstborn from the dead' means that as the 'second man' he is the head of a new humanity, so that all those who are raised from the dead into life, through faith in Jesus Christ, find him to be their leader or ruler, who gives them eternal life. But it is not simply the new humanity which is really important. Just as he was the agent of creation, so he will bring about a whole new created order. It is not only that we are going to be raised to eternal life, but that we shall inhabit new heavens and a new earth, in which righteousness will dwell.

As Christ's resurrection proves his supremacy over all of this, he is able to reconcile everything to himself (20). The whole created order is going to be brought into a right relationship with him. This whole fragmented, frustrated earth, as it is renewed, newly created by the risen Christ, will be reconciled to him. Both the destruction element, we saw in 2 Peter earlier, and the new creation element, we saw in Revelation 21, depend on this sovereign cosmic Christ, who is over everything, Lord above all. It is both humbling and enormously energising to realise that God has such amazing purposes for creation and for our part in it, which we often fail to see.

The 'now' and the 'not yet' in creation

As we begin to draw the threads together, we need to hold on to this dual role of Jesus Christ as creator and new creator, since it helps to fuse together the 'now' and 'not yet' of our Christian experience. We often separate them for teaching purposes, but we should think of the 'now' as being part of a continuous sequence into the 'not yet'. Christ as creator and king brings together what we already have in him with what we will have in eternity in Christ. He unites this creation with the new creation – the new heavens and the new earth.

The point in history at which the fusion occurred was when Christ was raised from the dead. Easter morning was in a very real sense the first day of a new creation, as C S Lewis described it. That point of fusion is how we know that this 'now' experience of Christ is going to lead us to the future heavenly glory with Christ. It is because God has raised him from the dead. At that moment, the life of the world to come for ever transformed the life of this world. That great event, which brought our

redemption – Jesus' death on the cross and God's vi
of his Son by raising him from the dead – that is the
reference point to which we must return, whenever we a..
tempted to doubt the reality of our future focus.

2. LIVING IN THE LIGHT OF HIS COMING

What do Christ's coming and the fulfilment of the new creation
mean for us in practical terms? Here are some applications to explore.

i. Be holy!

Dealing with Christ's return, in his second letter, Peter asks, 'What
kind of people ought you to be?' (2 Pet. 3:11) He answers this
question with the instruction, 'You ought to live holy and godly
lives as you look forward to the day of God and speed its coming.'

The logic is very clear. We are going to a holy city where
citizenship has become ours through the sacrificial death of our
holy Saviour. Offering his perfect righteousness in the place of
our sinful rebellion, he not only paid the price of our past
wickedness, but secured the imputation of his righteousness to
our account, as a free gift of God's grace, for ever. As rescued
people, is it possible for us to be anything less than passionate
about becoming 'like him', which is essentially what holiness is?
How can we ever sit light to sin, when we see both what it cost
our Saviour and also what a glorious future he has provided for
all his believing people?

Holiness is not an optional extra for honours candidates.
Holiness is what the Christian life is all about. We know that in
this life we shall always have to fight against the world, the flesh
and the devil. We know that we still have a wretched, sinful nature
that is not going to be transformed fully into his likeness until
we see him face to face. Therefore the Christian life is a fight
and a race to be run. But it is also a daily experience of God's

grace and power, through his Spirit living within us, changing us progressively into the likeness of the Lord Jesus.

One of the marks of genuine Christian discipleship is seen in our desire to become more like the Lord Jesus, so that we centre our lives on this great ambition. We must not be stumbled because 'holiness' has become a negative term, in the way the world uses it. One has only to think of the connotations of the phrase 'holier than thou'. The biblical terms holiness, godliness, sanctification, all mean growing into the likeness of the image of God, in Jesus Christ. 'Be holy as I am holy', says the Lord.

If we have begun to grasp something of our ultimate destination, we need to live now in the light of that reality, seeking to grow in godliness day by day. That means putting on the armour of light and fighting against the world, the flesh and the devil:

> The night is nearly over; the day is almost here, so let us put aside the deeds of darkness and put on the armour of light. Let us behave decently, as in the daytime, not in orgies and drunkenness, not in sexual immorality and debauchery, not in dissension and jealousy. Rather, clothe yourselves with the Lord Jesus Christ, and do not think about how to gratify the desires of the sinful nature (Rom. 13:12-14).

As we live in the light of his coming, we must put on the Lord Jesus Christ, clothe ourselves with him, put aside the deeds of darkness, and put on the armour of light. We must not even begin to think about how to gratify the desires of the sinful nature, because as soon as we start to think about it we shall want to do it, which is how temptation gets hold of us.

We are going to the holy city and God has redeemed us to be his holy people. That transformation will, of course, only come to its ultimate fulfilment when we see him face to face, but what an expectation we have!

> Dear friends, now we are children of God, and what we will be has not yet been made known. But we know that when he appears, we shall be like him, for we shall see him as he is. Everyone who has this hope in him purifies himself just as he is pure (1 John 3:2-3).

Here is another apostle, John, with the same concern. Since we are going to see him and we will be transformed into his likeness, how are we to live in the present before that great day? We purify ourselves. If Jesus has done all this for us, we should want to show our love for him by growing more like him day by day, and he has given us his Holy Spirit to enable us to change. If we really have heaven in our view, we shall want to arrive there with God's grace having worked as much of his transformation in us as is possible in this world. We have to apprehend and appreciate the gospel of grace every day to help us persevere with the work of holiness.

ii. Be faithful!

We are to be doing the Master's work while we are waiting for the Master to come. To demonstrate what this means very powerfully, we can go to the parables of Jesus in Matthew 24 and 25, where he immediately moves on from teaching about the *fact* of his coming to the need to be found faithful and ready for that day. Four of the group of five parables in Matthew 24:42-25:46 focus on the *delay* in Christ's coming, and emphasise the need for faithfulness and constructive servanthood as we wait. Think especially of the punch in the parable of the talents, with its clear message of reward and loss. These parables are very important in terms of setting the agenda of faithfulness in this world.

We should be motivated by whatever the eternal rewards may be without embarrassment. Christ is coming bringing his reward, and we can be motivated by the fact that nothing we do for the Lord Jesus in this world is ever lost (1 Cor. 15:58). It must be done for the Lord Jesus, because we love him and we are serving him. We are committed to doing the Master's work as faithfully as we can in the Master's strength. These are practical evidences of our understanding of the second coming: as we persevere in fighting the good fight, keeping up the good work, being faithful to the Master's purposes.

iii. **Be diligent!**

In studying the Thessalonian letters, we find that those early Christians had a real grasp of the vivid reality that Jesus was coming back. But some of them were apparently looking for financial support, so that they need not work, in order to focus their energy on being 'ready' for him. Paul was not impressed by this false piety. His riposte was that those who refused to work should not eat. It is an insight on lazy people who think it is spiritual to say, 'if Jesus is coming back, then I must prepare myself spiritually for his return and will you please provide me with some cash so that I can do it?'!

> In the name of the Lord Jesus Christ, we command you, brothers, to keep away from every brother who is idle and does not live according to the teaching you received from us. For you yourselves know how you ought to follow our example. We were not idle when we were with you, nor did we eat anyone's food without paying for it. On the contrary, we

worked night and day, labouring and toiling so
that we would not be a burden to any of you (2
Thess. 3:6).

In the context of Jesus coming back, they were required to
be diligent, hard workers, not idle slackers. The principle is very
important. The Christian who is truly living in the light of the
second coming will not be swanning around doing little of earthly
use, or spending all his time in speculation about the details. He
is working hard and diligently now. He is getting on with the
work God has given him to do, whatever that work may be. The
place where God has put us is the place *God* has put us, so we
need to get on with our work, and use it to serve him now. It is
as we are diligent in our present service of the Master, that we
demonstrate our faithfulness to him.

It is possible as a Christian to be a workaholic (which is
wrong), but we should be characterised as hard workers. Let us
not fall for the idea that the Christian life is an easy ride. Being a
Christian is hard work, but Christ is the one who gives us the
energy to keep on keeping on as we turn to him. He is also the
one who will show us if and when we are going far too hard,
and we must take notice of that too. Our commitment to Christ
carries with it a commitment to whatever God has given us to
do, because we are living in the light of eternity, and because we
know that in the eternal perspective God will be faithful in
rewarding those who have been faithful to him.

iv. Be joyful!

In Chapter 1, we looked at how faith is 'dancing to the music' of
our future hope now. We should have an attitude of joy as we go
about our master's work. Christ is concerned with all that happens
in his creation and is active in it: so should his people be. Rather
than being world-weary – although we do look forward to what

is to come – there is much that he has commissioned us to do now, using the gifts and talents he has given us. Knowing what we know, we can do all to the glory of God, and with joy and satisfaction.

This applies to our gospel ministry in the narrow sense of 'Christian work', but also to all the other spheres of human life and experience which belong to him: our families, science, education, the law, art. If he is redeeming us and redeeming creation, then we must realise that he has made us and our present environment for each other and for him. Heaven will be the extension and perfection of these good gifts of our faithful creator, only there, the joys will be more solid, and the treasures and satisfaction unfading, lasting as they will for eternity.

THE CHRISTIAN HOPE

Holiness, faithfulness, diligence and joy – these qualities should characterise our Christian experience in the here and now. Everything is going to find its fulfilment in our Lord Jesus Christ, the firstborn over all creation and the firstborn from among the dead, the ruler of the cosmos and the ruler of the church. As believers, we are in him now and for eternity, by grace through faith. We passionately want to remain in him and to grow in his likeness as we look forward to his coming again. Then our king will bring in the splendour of his kingdom, the new heavens and new earth – our unimaginable new environment – and we, as his new humanity, will reflect his glory, in all its brilliance. This, and nothing less, is the Christian hope. This is the gospel we must preach.

7.

Further Resources for Preaching on the Christian Hope

The aim of this book has been to act as a *starter* for the expositor, and as an encouragement to preach on this great theme of the Christian Hope. There are various resources available to help you further, including many biblical commentaries on the passages referred to in this book. In this section we draw attention to a few places that you might look for further help, but it should not be regarded as exhaustive, nor as a list of 'sound' or 'hallmarked' sources! Wide reading is to be encouraged. But neither time nor money is unlimited, and so it may help to make some suggestions here.

COMMENTARIES AND OTHER USEFUL THEOLOGICAL WORKS

As far as commentaries on the various biblical books are concerned, space forbids listing all those useful for this study. Suffice to say that it is generally wise to have one, or perhaps two, trusted conservative commentaries majoring on the *text* (as opposed to devotional commentaries) which can be relied upon to keep you on the straight and narrow. But on the other hand, one should never have too high an expectation of any commentary as far as helping the actual sermon is concerned. The clearest and soundest can be the driest and dullest! We would encourage reading anything you find on the bookshelf or can pick up cheaply, because often it may be just a single sentence from the most unlikely source that sparks the most fruitful thinking for the preacher.

Of the more thematic books on this subject, reference works such as *The Dictionary of the New Testament and Its Later Developments*, eds. R P Martin and P M Davids (IVP, 1997) and *The New Dictionary of Biblical Theology*, eds. B Rosner & TD Alexander (IVP, 2000) have some useful articles for reference. Larger treatments of the subject can be found in Anthony A Hoekema's *The Bible and The Future* (Paternoster, 1978), and also *The Meaning of the Millennium*, ed. Robert G Clouse (IVP USA, 1977), as well as *The Promise Of The Future* by Cornelis P Venema (Banner of Truth, 2000). The recent addition to the BST Bible Themes series by Bruce Milne, *The Message of Heaven and Hell*, (IVP, 2002) is an excellent and comprehensive work majoring on exposition of the material relating to heaven and hell as it comes right through the Bible. His earlier book, *The End of the World* (Kingsway, 1983) is much shorter, but also excellent. There are of course many other helpful books, but these would give the preacher a good start.

PROCLAMATION TRUST MEDIA RESOURCES

The main purpose of The Proclamation Trust is to encourage such expository preaching wherever we can, and particularly among those whose full-time calling is regular preaching of the word of God. To that end we hold regular preaching conferences for ministers, and run our own full-time course, the *Cornhill Training Course*, preparing people for Bible-teaching ministries. **PT Media** seeks to make our resources widely available to those in ministry throughout the United Kingdom and across the world, through a large audio ministry, video training materials, website resources and the printed word.

The following is just a small selection of the audio recordings we have on preaching this theme.

The Christian Hope:
5 expositions by David Jackman on eschatology given in a summer family conference setting. These include some of the contents of this book, though in a somewhat less comprehensive format.

Sceptics and the Advent of Christ:.
8 sermons on 2 Peter:3. Lunchtime talks to business men, by Dick Lucas.

What the future holds:
5 sermons from Mark 13, by Dick Lucas.

The Coming Day:
5 sermons on the second coming of Christ, by James Philip.

Heaven and Hell:
2 addresses by Bruce Milne from the Evangelical Ministry Assembly.

Jesus' Teaching on Hell:
4 short talks from Tuesday lunchtimes by Dick Lucas.

In addition, PT Media has hundreds of recordings covering all the biblical passages treated in this book, by a number of expositors. These are available from audio@proctrust.org.uk. Full catalogues of this and other material may be viewed at www.proctrust.org.uk where online ordering is available.

Appendix
Other Proclamation Trust Resources

PREACHING WORKSHOPS ON VIDEO

Even the most gifted preachers can learn together with others who share their calling, and preaching workshops can have a great impact on helping people nurture and develop their Bible teaching ability. These video materials provide resources for workshop groups among preachers or other Bible teachers. They can be used among ministers locally, students in college, or within congregations to train Bible teachers in differing contexts, including teaching the Bible to young people. We hope they may help excite a desire to preach God's Word as the answer to the greatest need in the church and the world today.

The Unashamed Workman: Instructions on biblical preaching

In Series 1, *The Unashamed Workman,* Dick Lucas distils decades of experience as an expositor into four lectures of 'instructions' that focus the approach to the Bible. Dick Lucas is Rector Emeritus of St Helen's Bishopsgate, London and was the founding chairman of The Proclamation Trust.

Meeting Jesus: Preaching from the Gospels

In Series 2, *Meeting Jesus*, David Jackman focuses particularly on preaching from the four Gospels. David Jackman is Director of the *Cornhill Training Course*.

Each series is a self-contained, fully integrated resource with four video lectures, material for further group work, and guidance for leaders on how to set up and run a preaching group. Both use worked examples to illustrate basic principles of exposition, model it in their own approach to the text, and give further material to work through in groups to drive the message home. Each workshop set comprises the videos, plus the *Leader's manual* and one copy of the *Preacher's Workbook*. Further copies of the latter, which contains the lecture notes and guidance for workshop preparation, should be ordered for all members of the group. Further details are available on the PT website.

OTHER AUDIO RESOURCES

We have a very extensive catalogue of expository ministry, both sermons and conference addresses. Most is available on cassette tape, and selected materials are also in digital audio format (MP3). Fully searchable catalogue programme can be downloaded from the website, and there are also online catalogues in *pdf* format and as excel spreadsheets which are readable on most computers. Full details of sales and loan services are available online.

PREACHING CONFERENCES

PT runs about twelve conferences each year, primarily for those in full-time preaching ministries, but also for lay preachers and Bible teachers, students and wives of ministers. The largest by far is the annual **Evangelical Ministry Assembly**, held in London each June. Most of the other conferences are residential, and involve work in small preaching workshop groups as well as main expositions. Details of all these, and booking facilities, can be found on the website.

CORNHILL TRAINING COURSE

The course runs either full-time over one year, or part-time over two years. It is aimed primarily at those intending to enter full-time preaching ministries, but we also have some places for those wanting to train for other areas of Bible teaching ministry, such as youth and children's work and ministry among women. Further details are on the website.

The ***Cornhill Summer School***, a one-week intensive course on Bible handling with practical teaching training runs in early July.

Details of all PT Media resources, conferences and the Cornhill Training Course are available on the Proclamation Trust website **www.proctrust.org.uk**. For further information on any of The Proclamation Trust's ministries, contact the head office.

Willcox House,
140-148 Borough High Street,
London SE1 1LB.
t +44 (0)207 407 0561
f +44 (0)207 407 0569

e pt@proctrust.org.uk
www.proctrust.org.uk

Other books of interest
from
Christian Focus
and
The Proclamation Trust

TEACHINGJOHN

unlocking the gospel of john for the expositor

PROCLAMATION
TRUST MEDIA

DICK**LUCAS**
WILLIAM**PHILIP**

Teaching John

Unlocking the Gospel of John for the Expositor

Dick Lucas and William Philip

Preachers find themselves turning to John's Gospel time and time again to proclaim its wonderful message about Jesus. This primer explores the main themes of John's own preaching of Christ, the Son of God, as preserved in the book he wrote for us.

John makes clear his own key purpose in writing in chapter 20 of his Gospel, and this stated intention must guide the exposition of his words today. It gives a way into the text so the Christian preacher may expound the message as John himself intended he should.

Many commentaries are written on John, but few focus directly on the needs of the preacher and congregation. This book is aimed precisely there. John's own key is used to unlock four famous chapters of his Gospel from the preacher's perspective, and with the sermon in clear view. The goal is to whet the preacher's appetite for teaching John today.

Dick Lucas is chairman of The Proclamation Trust, which exists to train and encourage preachers in expository ministry. He is Rector Emeritus of St Helen's Church, Bishopsgate, where his four decades of ministry centred on thorough exposition of the Scriptures to congregations of businessmen, students and other young people.

William Philip directs the general ministry of the Proclamation Trust.

ISBN 1-85792-790-7

DAVID**JACKMAN**
WILLIAM**PHILIP**

PROCLAMATION
TRUST MEDIA

TEACHING**MATTHEW**

unlocking the gospel of matthew for the expositor

Teaching Matthew

Unlocking the Gospel of Matthew for the Expositor

David Jackman and William Philip

Matthew's Gospel is a substantial book - its large sections on teaching and theological reflection seeming to predominate over the 'action' of the story. However, precisely because there are such rich seams of theology, and so much teaching from Jesus himself, it is a wonderful treasure-trove.

It also excels as a way of explaining the message of the New Testament gospel so as to open up a sense of its *continuity* with the whole Old Testament, and the *fulfilment* of God's covenant promises in Jesus Christ.

Though principally aimed at preachers who are preparing expository sermons, *Teaching Matthew* will help Bible teachers in a variety of settings as well as those simply reading Matthew for themselves.

Each chapter ends with a brief conclusion to help crystallise your thinking.

David Jackman is the President of the Proclamation Trust and Director of the Cornhill Training Course, London, England, whose aims are the effective communication of the gospel, especially through preaching. Previously he was the minister of Above Bar Church, Southampton.

William Philip directs the general ministry of the Proclamation Trust

ISBN 1-85792-877-6

mentor

Preaching
the
Living Word

**Addresses from the
Evangelical Ministry Assembly**

'These superb addresses are the pick of the crop.
They are absolute gold dust.'

Wallace Benn, Bishop of Lewes

Dick Lucas, Alec Motyer, J. I. Packer,
Peter Jensen, Bruce Milne,
Mark Ashton and David Jackman

Preaching the Living Word

Addresses from the Evangelical Ministry Assembly

Edited by David Jackman

Dick Lucas, Alec Motyer, J.I. Packer, Bruce Milne, Peter Jensen, David Jackman, Mark Ashton

'These superb addresses are the pick of the crop. They are absolute gold dust. I recommend this book enthusiastically and with joy.'
Wallace Benn, Bishop of Lewes

'This compilation of carefully edited addresses is an excellent sampler of the Assembly itself. More than that it provides the kind of instructive teaching and preaching which will serve to strengthen the ministry of the Word of God everywhere.'
Dr. Sinclair B. Ferguson,
Westminster Seminary, Dallas Campus, Texas

'This excellent book is a joy to read... it wonderfully captures the feel of the assembly.'
Dr. Paul Gardner, Rural Dean, Hartford, Cheshire

In this book you will discover:-

    --   How to make preaching more effective
    --   How to restore its centrality to worship in the Church
    --   How to structure Bible exposition
    --   How to preach from different parts of Scripture
    --   How to preach doctrine

This is not a book about style, but how to extract the best from the Word of God when delivering a message.

ISBN 1-85792-312-X

EDITED**BY**
WILLIAM**PHILIP**

THE
PRACTICAL**PREACHER**

practical wisdom for the pastor-teacher

contributions by:
MELVIN**TINKER** • DAVID**JACKMAN** • MARTIN**ALLEN**
JONATHAN**PRIME** • SINCLAIR**FERGUSON**

The Practical Preacher

Practical Wisdom for the Pastor – Teacher

Edited by William J U Philip

Melvin Tinker, David Jackman, Martin Allen, Jonathan Prime, Sinclair Ferguson

How do we approach with godly wisdom the task of being a pastor-teacher in Christ's church? We must preach the word; but if we take seriously the New Testament injunctions about how we address this primary task, we will show our wisdom by humility, a teachable spirit, and diligence in pursuing all profitable means to present ourselves approved and unashamed workmen of God (2 Tim. 2:15).

Many questions face us:

-- How do you introduce biblical exposition where it has been previously unknown?
-- How do you plan an effective preaching programme?
-- What distinguishes truly biblical ministry from merely 'bible-based' ministry?
-- Do we properly understand and relate to the real people that make up our congregations, both personally and theologically?

This book gives practical help in these areas for those seeking to develop authentic biblical expository ministry. Each contributor is totally committed to this priority, and each writes from the perspective of biblical reflection and real experience in local church ministry.

Only the already-perfect pastor has nothing to learn from its pages!

ISBN-1 85792-794-X

Christian Focus Publications

We publish books for all ages. Our mission statement -
STAYING FAITHFUL
In dependence upon God we seek to help make his infallible
word, the Bible, relevant. Our aim is to ensure that the Lord
Jesus Christ is presented as the only hope to obtain forgiveness
of sin, live a useful life and look forward to heaven with him.

REACHING OUT
Christ's last command requires us to reach out to our world with
his gospel. We seek to help fulfil that by publishing books that
point people towards Jesus and for them to develop a Christ-
like maturity. We aim to equip all levels of readers for life, work,
ministry and mission.

Books in our adult range are published in three imprints:-
Christian Focus contains popular works including biographies,
commentaries, basic doctrine, and Christian living. Our
children's books are also published in this imprint.
Christian Heritage contains classic writings from the past.
Mentor focuses on books written at a level suitable for Bible
College and seminary students, pastors, and other serious
readers; the imprint includes commentaries, doctrinal studies,
examination of current issues, and church history.
We can be contacted at:
Christian Focus Publications, Ltd
Geanies House, Fearn,
Ross-shire, IV20 1TW, Scotland,
United Kingdom
info@christianfocus.com

For details of our titles visit us on our website
www.christianfocus.com